*Learning and Teaching Practices
in English*

THE LIBRARY OF EDUCATION

A Project of The Center for Applied Research in Education, Inc.

G. R. Gottschalk, Director

Categories of Coverage

I	II	III
Curriculum and Teaching	Administration, Organization, and Finance	Psychology for Educators

IV	V	VI
History, Philosophy, and Social Foundations	Professional Skills	Educational Institutions

Learning and Teaching Practices
in English

GENEVA HANNA PILGRIM

The University of Texas

The Center for Applied Research in Education, Inc.

New York

THE CENTER FOR APPLIED
RESEARCH IN EDUCATION, INC.
NEW YORK

LIBRARY OF CONGRESS
CATALOG CARD NO.: 66–13406

PRINTED IN THE UNITED STATES OF AMERICA

Foreword

Most American adults have been through at least part of the mill of public education. Paramount in their school memories is that subject called English. For some, the memories are pleasant and exciting—the thrill of finding the exact combination of words to pin down an elusive idea or of the world of enchantment and ideas they discovered in literature. For more, the memories are probably unpleasant ones of playing an incomprehensible game in which apparently only the teacher knew the rules. They struggled with the mysteries of grammar and never found the secret; they desperately tried to make words fall in correct patterns but were always wrong; they read of unreal people who performed unreal acts that the teacher always professed had a meaning they did not see.

As adults, they have come to a realization of the inadequacies of their own language skills. They now feel that there must be answers to the problems that trouble them about their own inner lives. So they say, "Take our children. Teach them to write; teach them to read; teach them to spell; teach them to speak clearly and well. Please help them to live richer lives than we do." These requests seemingly impose a simple task on the public schools, and certainly teachers of English should be capable of doing these simple things in a straightforward manner.

Dr. Pilgrim's book does a masterful job of showing the complexities the school faces in trying to achieve these goals. She presents in clear and straightforward prose the complexity of the social order, the complexity within the individual child as he struggles toward maturity, the complexity of the differences that exist between individuals of the same chronological age, and the complexity of the subject matter itself.

Dr. Pilgrim has presented many of the patterns in which English is organized in the schools today. These are carefully defined, and—

more important—the reasoning that led to their establishment is objectively presented. Throughout the book, there is a careful evaluation of both the strengths and weaknesses inherent in various approaches.

The book should be of real service to students who want a bird's-eye view of English in the schools today, and it should be of particular service to lay persons concerned with their schools and where they are going.

G. ROBERT CARLSEN
Professor of English and Education
State University of Iowa
Iowa City, Iowa

Learning and Teaching Practices in English

by Geneva Hanna Pilgrim

The basic course of study in all secondary schools is that of the English curriculum. Probably no other set of courses has the long term value to the student as does that of the English program. *Learning and Teaching Practices in English* by Geneva Hanna Pilgrim is a thorough view of the English program used in American public secondary schools. This book covers grades 7 through 12 in its scope, all aspects of the English program in depth, and the practices of the country in variety. The book is carefully written. It includes a number of descriptions of English education practices garnered from a variety of schools in the country.

The book begins with a discussion of the English curriculum together with the nature of language. It proceeds to discuss a number of basic approaches in the teaching of English: such as the functional and grammatical unit aproaches. A significant chapter on the teaching of English treats in some detail the various problems of team teaching; grouping; teaching the low-achiever, the academically talented, and the average. Newer topics, such as teaching English as a second language, and teaching the emotionally disturbed are included in this chapter. Dr. Pilgrim discusses in separate chapters the teaching of English in grades 7, 8 and 9, and English in grades 10, 11 and 12. Here she attempts to get at the problems of the learner as well as problems in content in the field. Her concern is with these two topics as they relate to the teaching of English in these two organizational units.

The final chapter is an interesting one dealing with special problems incurred by changing trends in the teaching of English. Each of the special areas—literature, grammar, speaking, spelling and so on—is treated separately. Both the problems and present trends are taken into account.

Learning and Teaching Practices in English is a book which gives an over-view of the English curriculum in the American public school. Being comprehensive and well-written, it is a contribution to the literature of this field.

DANIEL E. GRIFFITHS
Content Editor

Contents

CHAPTER I

Background: The "What" and "Why" of English in Secondary Schools

No educator seriously questions the position of English in the curriculum. With the exception of American history, no other subject is universally required for graduation from high school. The reasons for this seem self-evident. Because nearly all of man's civilized activities depend upon language for interpretation, enrichment, and extension, a high degree of verbal ability is imperative if the individual is to function adequately in his society. It seems apparent, then, that one of the more important tasks of the school, as the chief educational agency of American culture, is to assist its young people in developing communication skills. The English curriculum is chiefly responsible for this development.

Brief History of the English Curriculum

In spite of this acceptance of English as a basic course, there are wide differences of opinion as to precisely what does or should constitute the content of the course at various levels. Perhaps a sketch of the history of the English curriculum in the secondary schools of the United States will help give some perspective on these differences.

The Latin Grammar Schools, the first form of secondary education in this country, concentrated on Latin, Greek, and mathematics. Occasionally a course in rhetoric, with special emphasis on oratory and the writing of elegant prose, was also offered. Literature, as it is now taught in the secondary schools, was seldom included. After one finished the elementary school, where reading was taught every year, it was assumed that one could read whatever came to hand and that instruction in literature, except as it pertained to figures of speech and specialized aspects of literary style, was unnecessary. When literature was studied, it was usually the writings of Homer,

Cicero, or Caesar (in the original) for purposes of language study.

However, a few secondary schools did begin to include literature as a subject early in the nineteenth century. In fact, the Boston Public High School, which opened in 1821, included English literature as one of the subjects in its curriculum.[1] As America prospered early in the nineteenth century, more and more young men and women wished to improve their lot through education. This led to the establishment of academies and public high schools which had as one of their objectives the preparation of young people to enter business and some of the minor professions without going to college. English literature, and later American literature, was generally included in the curriculums of these schools.

Many of the young people who attended these schools had meager cultural backgrounds. Some had difficulty expressing themselves in writing. As a consequence, in 1869 Harvard College added the writing of an essay to its college entrance requirements in order to ascertain whether or not the candidate could write, spell, and punctuate acceptable prose. Essay topics were drawn from a list of literary works published in the college catalog. In the 1869–70 catalog, two books—*Julius Caesar* and *Comus*—were named as alternates for the examination. In 1873–74 the requirements read as follows:

> *English Composition.* Each candidate will be required to write a short English composition, correct in spelling, punctuation, grammar, and expression, the subject to be taken from such works of standard authors as shall be announced from time to time. The subject for 1874 will be taken from one of the following works: Shakespeare's *Tempest, Julius Caesar,* and *Merchant of Venice;* Goldsmith's *Vicar of Wakefield;* Scott's *Ivanhoe,* and *Lay of the Last Minstrel.*[2]

Hosic reports that knowledge of literature for its own sake was introduced by Yale University in 1894, and this point of view was quickly adopted by other institutions. Uniform college entrance requirements, however, were not adopted even in New England until after the Committee of Ten made its report in 1894. The National Conference on Uniform Entrance Requirements in English, formed

---

[1] Elwood P. Cubberley, *Readings in Public Education in the United States* (Boston: Houghton Mifflin Company, 1934), p. 230.

[2] James Fleming Hosic (compiler), *Reorganization of English in Secondary Schools,* Bulletin No. 2 (Washington, D.C.: USGPO, 1917), p. 12.

in 1894, met at three- or four-year intervals for some years. Hosic further states that this group

> ... selected lists of books for reading and study in the preparatory school, to which were appended certain aims of English study and directions concerning the examinations to be set. . . . In February 1916 an alternative "comprehensive" plan was instituted, by which all candidates taking college entrance examinations should have the option of choosing questions not requiring a knowledge of certain prescribed books.[3]

As long as college board examinations included questions on specific literary selections, this practice helped to establish certain selections as "classics" which every educated young person should have read. Stout, in a history of the development of the high school in the North Central States, says:

> The ten years following 1890 show a rapid development in this kind of work. . . . There was lack of uniformity both in the number and character of the classics read, but this kind of material had come into general use. College entrance requirements no doubt exerted an influence in the direction of securing some degree of uniformity, but even these lacked uniformity practically until the close of the century.[4]

The following list shows the relative frequency with which some of the masterpieces appeared in the lists of the various schools. The ranking, in order of the ten most often named, is as follows:

1. *Merchant of Venice*
2. *Julius Caesar*
3. *Bunker Hill Oration*
4. *The Sketch Book*
4. *Evangeline*
4. *Vision of Sir Launfal*
5. *Snowbound*
6. *Macbeth*
7. *Lady of the Lake*
8. *Hamlet*
9. *Deserted Village*
10. Gray's *Elegy*
10. *Thanatopsis*
10. *As You Like It*

These works appear in the reading lists of more than 25 per cent of the schools; the one ranking first is found in nearly 70 per cent of the lists.[5]

Stout also gives the selections listed in 25 per cent or fewer of

---

[3] *Ibid.*, p. 13.
[4] John Elbert Stout, *The Development of High-School Curricula in the North Central States from 1860 to 1918* (Chicago: The University of Chicago Press, 1921), p. 137.
[5] *Ibid.*, p. 137.

the schools. Ranking fourth on this latter list are *Ivanhoe* and *Silas Marner.*[6]

Although today specific questions on certain literary works have disappeared altogether from these examinations, their influence is still present in our secondary school English programs. The poems of Longfellow are still read extensively in many junior high schools, as are *Julius Caesar, Hamlet, Silas Marner,* and *Ivanhoe* in senior high schools.

English grammar became part of the secondary curriculum during the latter part of the eighteenth century and the early part of the nineteenth century. Latin grammar had been taught extensively. Lyman describes the transition from Latin grammar to English grammar:

> In the Latin school the backbone of the course had been grammar; the term *grammar,* the method of teaching grammar were ingrained. Latin grammar had stood for the next step above reading and writing the vernacular. . . . when, therefore, the advocates of a practical English training (in the American colonies) found English grammar in Dilworth and other texts, what was more natural than that they would seize upon it as a suitable substitute for the next step above reading and writing and spelling? English they found reduced to the same accidence as Latin; textbooks informed them on title pages that grammar was the art of speaking and writing the English language correctly, and this was their laudable desire for their children; here is a suitable setting in the vernacular program for grammar as the basic study. This conviction made its way into legal sanction for English and English grammar in the last decade of the eighteenth century.[7]

Little attention was paid to the fact that English is not a Romance language, basically, nor that it is not as highly inflected as Latin. The structure and the terminology of Latin grammar have persisted in English grammar in spite of the endeavors of some textbook writers during the 1930's and 1940's to simplify the terms and make them more meaningful. Until recently, very little change had taken place in the content or the methods of teaching grammar. However, the modern linguists' approach to the study of language structure

---

[6] *Ibid.*, p. 138.

[7] Rollo L. Lyman, *English Grammar in American Schools Before 1850,* U.S. Office of Education Bulletin No. 12 (Washington, D.C.: USGPO, 1921), pp. 76, 77.

through analysis of the spoken language or sentence patterns has begun to have some effect.

Linguistics, as defined in the *American College Dictionary,* is:

> . . . the science of language, including among its fields phonetics, phonemics, morphology, and syntax, and having as principal divisions descriptive linguistics, which treats the classification and arrangement of the features of language, and comparative . . . linguistics, which treats linguistic change, especially by the study of data taken from various languages. . . .

This definition, however, has had but little effect on the study of English as a language in the secondary schools. This science is a newcomer to the fields of knowledge although there have been several outstanding men during the last hundred years pointing the way for the development of modern linguistics.

Changes in Secondary Education

At the turn of the twentieth century, English was part of almost all secondary school curriculums. Some literature ("standard" works), Latin grammar (applied to English), and rhetoric were included in the courses.

The first part of the twentieth century was to bring many changes to the secondary schools of America, and more changes were in store in the years ahead. With the enactment of child-labor laws, the compulsory school-attendance age was raised, so that most children were kept in school until the eighth grade. Gradually the minimum age has been raised in most states to at least sixteen. These laws have put more and more children into the public secondary schools. In the first half of the century, the secondary school population consisted of a relatively small number of students, most of whom planned to go on to college. In the 1920's, 1930's, and 1940's the number of secondary school students increased, but only a small percentage planned to go on to higher education. This picture has shifted somewhat since 1950. An even larger number of young people are attending high school, and an increased number (40–60 per cent) are going on to college. If this trend continues, it will mean that before the end of this century most young people will finish high school and many will go on to college.

This trend puts a large burden on the teaching of English, because communication is the key to success in academic learning. The student must be able to read with great speed and comprehension, as well as write and speak with accuracy and effectiveness. These skills cannot be learned with sufficient effectiveness in the elementary school; they must be taught continuously through high school and even into college.

The high school program, however, should never be completely college preparatory, for our society believes that it is important for young people to stay in school and requires them by law to do so. There will always be those who—for lack of ability, opportunity, or inclination—do not go on to higher education. The Commission on Human Resources and Advanced Training projected estimated enrollments to 1968–69:

> . . . the percentage of high school graduates entering college will not increase during this period, so that the ratio of high school graduates who will enroll in college will stabilize at about 35 per cent.[8]

In this same study the researchers estimated that the percentage of young people who will graduate from high school will increase, reaching 70 per cent by 1968. "Thus the ratio of the youth in the total population who go to college will, consequently, increase, approaching one-fourth of the appropriate age group by that date."[9] These data have real significance for teachers of English.

The knowledge teachers now have about adolescents and learning is another area of change. Developmental stages of growth have been observed and carefully studied to ascertain patterns of behavior. This type of research is still being carried on extensively. Several conclusions about adolescence are commonly accepted. There are sex differences in relation to learning—the effects of anxiety on learning language skills, for example, differ between boys and girls.[10] Interests in the early periods of adolescence also

---

[8] William M. Alexander and J. Galen Saylor, *Modern Secondary Education: Basic Principles and Practices* (New York: Holt, Rinehart & Winston, Inc., 1960), p. 66.

[9] *Ibid.*, p. 66.

[10] Olive Scarborough, Edwin Hindsman, and Geneva Hanna, "Anxiety Level and Performance in School Subjects," *Psychological Reports* (Missoula, Montana: Southern Universities Press, 1961), pp. 9, 425–30.

differ sharply according to sex. Norvell[11] found that sex was the most important factor in the differences in reading preferences between boys and girls. Girls generally prefer romance and sentiment in their literature, shunning the brutal and blood-and-thunder. Boys prefer adventure and excitement in which male characters predominate; they dislike sentiment and too much romance. Boys seldom like "girls'" books, but girls often like "boys'" books. These findings are highly significant for the English curriculum.

Psychologists have also found that adolescents are a volatile age group. Adolescents are changing physically and maturing rapidly. New physical drives may make them feel very insecure and, therefore, become quite unstable in behavior. Glandular adjustments affect emotional stability. They may be moody or wound up tight and in perpetual motion. Or they may be withdrawn and morose, seemingly too tired to keep awake in class or to pick up one foot after the other. Horseplay among adolescents—both boys and girls —is common. They often talk and laugh at the tops of their voices, yet when confronted with a question in the classroom they often cannot be heard two feet away. A sense of humor is necessary on the part of adults working with adolescents if they are to preserve their sanity!

The seeking of peer status is also characteristic of the American adolescent. The average youth is more desirous of being accepted and approved by his age mates than by his parents or teachers. This is not to say these young people do not also feel the need of good adult relationships, but these no longer dominate. Adolescents may lie or steal to "prove" themselves to the crowd, or they may conduct themselves in exemplary manner if that is in accord with the mores of the group.

Books may be read because "the crowd" is reading them, or simply because it is the thing to do. On the other hand, no books may be read because this is considered "too high-brow" by the peer group to which the adolescent belongs. Certain topics are taboo and others overused in oral or written discussions.

The one thing no adolescent—and perhaps no adult—in our culture can tolerate is to be ignored. To be disregarded, to feel no one cares whether he is around or not, to be left out—this is a state of

---

[11] George W. Norvell, *The Reading Interests of Young People* (Boston: D. C. Heath & Company, 1950).

existence completely abhorrent to the adolescent. He would rather be actively rejected by his peers than to be isolated by them or from them. Antisocial behavior is often caused by the feeling of being left out. At least someone will notice him if he misbehaves—if only to throw rocks at him.

Most adolescents are overtly or covertly seeking some purpose in life. Many become confused over religion—what is "right" or "wrong," what the world is all about, and where they fit into the whole complex pattern. Young people, given the chance and constructive encouragement, are idealists. (Witness the dedication of those who have joined the Peace Corps.) Unfortunately, our culture is so constituted that there is relatively little actual service young people can perform for their communities.

Indifference is a pose taken by many adolescents to cover up their feelings of inadequacy or their fear of ridicule. Boys, especially, hide their emotions because they are afraid of appearing sentimental and, therefore, weak and "sissy." If the adult working with these indifferent young people is patient as well as perceptive, his work will bear fruit. As adolescents begin to feel more secure, they will usually turn to constructive endeavors and often push themselves toward a mature concept of life and their place in it.

An important characteristic of adolescents is the extreme individual differences to be found among them. Starting with the obvious physical differences in development between the sexes, we find girls of twelve to fifteen one to two years ahead of boys in physical development. Girls are generally taller and often heavier than boys their age. Within the sexes there is wide variation in normal patterns of growth. In eighth- or ninth-grade classrooms, it is not uncommon to see a little boy who is shorter than any of the girls and who has not started to mature physically alongside a boy six feet four who obviously is sexually and physically quite mature. This same phenomenon may be observed in the girls.

If the physical variations seem extreme, they are nothing compared to the differences in learning abilities. There are the fast and the slow, the brilliant and the dull, the ambitious and the lazy, those talented or handicapped in a special way, the mature readers and the nonreaders, the loquacious and the silent. These are only a few of the areas in which adolescents differ.

The United States has been built on the very concept of diversity.

Democracy, as a form of government and as a way of life, demands respect for the individual and emphasis on uniqueness. Our continued strength as a nation depends upon our ability to capitalize on the many variations inherent in our youth and to utilize and develop each person's peculiar capacities to the utmost.

This concept presents a real challenge to the teacher of English. Because nearly all the educable adolescents are in secondary school, and because all are required to take English, meeting the needs of these diverse human beings as well as capitalizing on their differences takes all of the knowledge, skill, and ingenuity an adult can muster.

The Nature of Language

Language is the chief means of communication among human beings. Without it, life would have very little meaning; learning would be very difficult; and we would not be able to pass on the thoughts and ideas of one generation to the next. The concept of verbal symbols is an amazing achievement and one of the more important characteristics distinguishing the human being from the rest of the animal world.

Without language there would be no history or any planning for the future. There would be no vicarious experience; all experience would have to be firsthand. The experiences in which we do participate would have a much narrower meaning. Through language we associate the past with the present; we can project, making predictions for the future based on the past and present. Abstraction and conceptualization would be impossible without language.

There are those who say: "You are your language"—which is to say that, as a person develops, he learns to respond verbally with certain individual patterns to the stimulus of his environment. These responses may or may not be appropriate to the situation, but they are *his* ways of expressing his feelings and reactions. Patterns of language use are developed which become characteristic of the individual as well as of the language. Personality is revealed through word choice and sentence patterns, as well as by tone of voice or facial expression. If one is characteristically happy or morose, flippant or derisive, his language will reveal it. Every time he opens his mouth or writes a sentence, he reveals himself.

Personality is reflected in the receptive acts of communication as well as in speaking and writing. The way in which one interprets or responds to what he hears or sees on the written page will show rather quickly the kind of person he is. If he is defensive or easily hurt, he often misinterprets the statements of others. On the other hand, if he is secure and compassionate, he will interpret what he hears in as positive, yet realistic, a manner as possible.

Most of the good things in life are enhanced by and through language. The poet sees a field of daffodils and writes a poem which enables hundreds of others to recall similar sights. The dramatist takes a problem involving conflict and makes his audience feel the pull and tug of the opposing ideas as dramatized by the actors. A humorous situation is made twice as funny through the clever words used by a master storyteller.

The emotions are both stimulated and released through language. Anguish is often alleviated by pouring out one's grief to a sympathetic friend. Anger can be increased or assuaged through words. A glow of well-being may occur as a result of praise for a job well done. Love between two people is strengthened by verbal expressions of the mutual feeling.

No one person can see or feel or taste all there is of any situation. Hearing what others see or understand from similar circumstances may open our eyes to things we had never seen before. Thus language is necessary for the expansion of knowledge within the individual or the group.

Language is more than words or a vocabulary; it is the patterning of thought and ideas into symbols—expressions that will have an impact on the thinking and feelings of others. Demagogues learn the art of emotional appeal through language and thus control a large populace. Great writers, and even rather mediocre ones, have a talent for putting experience into words so vivid that the reader relives the scene and feels fear, love, or hate along with the characters. Thomas Paine's *Common Sense* is given credit for arousing many colonists against the British in the early years of the American Revolution. Harriet Beecher Stowe's *Uncle Tom's Cabin,* although far from being a literary masterpiece, has been given much credit by historians for stirring up the North against slavery.

Language in a Democracy

Literacy—the ability to read and write a language—has been the aim of most elementary education for centuries. Without these skills the individual is handicapped, no matter how bright he may be. Man has recognized this for centuries. Because we know that language has power, we want everyone to have access to language tools and skills. Without a literate population, the democratic form of government cannot survive. People who are responsible for decision-making must possess the tools for gaining adequate information.

At the opening of World War II, Germany and Japan had the highest rates of literacy of any of the nations in the world. But literacy for what? To follow a dictator and to learn to hate? To be brainwashed with distorted facts with little or no access to other facts?

Unfortunately, we sometimes become so concerned with the skills that we forget the true purpose behind their attainment. We often fail to appreciate the great responsibility these broadened avenues of communication put upon the individual if they are to be used constructively rather than destructively. Schools thus have an obligation to teach positive, constructive uses of these skills if Americans are to fulfill their roles in a democracy.

The teacher is faced with the further responsibility for giving direction to language learning consistent with certain principles compatible with democratic ideals. If critical thinking is important to democratic ideals, if the method of intelligence as opposed to "might makes right" is imperative to the democratic process, then the English teacher in American schools has great responsibility for teaching the skills of language through the processes of critical thinking.

With this point of view, it is easy to make English a handmaiden to all the other disciplines. The learning of reading and writing, speaking and listening, can be done through the content of many subject areas. There should be some emphasis of communication skills in every classroom as the need arises. The development of vocabulary, correct spelling, special problems of reading certain materials, and good usage patterns are the responsibility of every good teacher regardless of subject matter. These language skills are important for efficient learning of every content field.

The "What" of English

The fact that language is used and learned in every classroom of the secondary school does not obviate the need, however, for special instruction in the communication arts. Just what should English, as a subject area, include? Is it merely the skills of communication? These skills are an important part of the English curriculum, but only a part. Learning where and how to collect information for an informal class report, how to organize it in a meaningful and interesting manner either in writing or orally, and how to present it effectively is an activity which certainly should be a part of every English program. Another part of the English program is experimenting with language in order to express one's deepest feelings or wildest imaginings and receiving thoughtful, appreciative reactions to these attempts at creativity. Learning to read a newspaper intelligently, to discriminate between the trash and the good in magazines on the newsstands, to pass informed critical judgment on television programs and movies are important materials for the English class. It is also necessary to develop a liking and an appreciation for literature of various types.

All of this and more is an essential part of every young person's education. This is English as an academic study, not merely a language. An effective English course serves every phase of life and living, but it also has a unique content consisting of literature, language structure, and imaginative writing.

Because English as a language is such an essential tool in living and learning, no one needs to be defensive about the study of English in our secondary schools. The real problem is to know precisely what content should be included and how it should be organized. New knowledge is being discovered and produced constantly and at a tremendous rate. If the new is to be incorporated, then some of the old must be discarded.

What guidelines are there for decision-making on content? Five criteria are evident from the foregoing discussion of the nature of language and the nature of adolescents.

1. *Language is individual; therefore, each student should be given an opportunity to express himself and his uniqueness.* This implies a permissive atmosphere in the classroom wherein honest diversity is encouraged. Students are frequently startled at their own

progress when they are stimulated and allowed freedom of honest expression. Charming poetry has been written, sparkling repartee has been produced, interesting stories have been told by young people who were just discovering themselves. All content will be expected to produce some conformity, of course, as in punctuation or spelling. This is a minor part of the English program, however, and can easily be balanced by allowing freedom of expression.

2. *Language is a social instrument; therefore, content should have social worth.* There should be some constructive purpose in all content offered in the English class. This does not mean a saccharin attitude toward literature and literary topics, but it does mean that the values implied as well as expressed should be compatible with the best in the culture. This eliminates the overly sentimental as well as the needlessly brutal and sadistic. Although the audience witnesses cruelty and brutality in a performance of *King Lear,* there is social purpose behind the plot: the brutality is understood, but not condoned. The audience has compassion for Lear because of the cruel treatment he receives, and perhaps each one sees a bit of himself in the selfish, inhuman daughters. Compassion and identification of one's own defects are important learnings if the adolescent is to become a mature adult.

Students should be held responsible for what they write and say. The right of free speech is not a license to speak untruths or half-truths, nor does it guarantee immunity to adverse consequences if the individual offends others by what he says or writes. Language always carries implications of responsibility toward others.

3. *English content should serve the major purposes of American education.* According to The Commission on the English Curriculum of the National Council of the Teachers of English, there are three major purposes of American education:

> (1) Cultivation of satisfying and wholesome personal lives; (2) development of social sensitivity and effective participation in the life of the local community, the nation, and the world; and (3) preparation for vocational competence.[12]

Now, as never before, young people must be made aware of American ideals. Inherent in these ideals is the right of every young

---

[12] The Commission on the English Curriculum of The National Council of Teachers of English, *The English Language Arts* (New York: Appleton-Century-Crofts, Inc., © 1952), pp. 6–7. Reprinted by permission of Appleton-Century-Crofts.

person to develop his own capacities to the fullest, and thus to live a more satisfying life. By the same token, the student should become aware of his responsibilities to himself, his friends and family, the local community, the nation, and the world. To assume these responsibilities, he must be able to think straight and act rationally.

Developing vocational competence is a major goal of many students. The English class should assist each individual in developing those skills and language competencies he will need most in his work. Adequate preparation for further academic work may be the best possible preparation for a vocation as well. All jobs, except perhaps the most routine or unskilled, demand a degree of communication skill. One must be able to understand directions, to make reports, to converse with one's fellow workers. Inadequate skills in listening or speaking or in reading or writing may cost a man his job or, at least, a promotion. Conversely, above-average communication skills—the ability to mix well with all kinds of people, to report intelligently on one's work or on a suggestion for improvement of operations, to understand what others have done and be able to make appropriate applications to one's situation—are also vocational skills which must be taken into consideration when evaluating the English curriculum.

4. *The content or knowledge to be learned should be as accurate and as up to date as possible.* The English language is in a state of constant change. This change keeps it dynamic and functional in serving American society. Too frequently English content has been based on what the teacher herself learned in high school. Many teachers of English see no relationship between the linguistics course they had in college and the Latin grammar they teach in the high school. Tradition dominates the curriculum. Verbals have always been taught in the ninth grade so that is where they are placed, without much question as to their importance to the language of ninth-graders as it is spoken and written, to say nothing of questioning the authenticity of continuing to teach the sins of the split infinitive.

It is equally important to have the highest quality of material available for the purposes desired. Literary selections are all too frequently included because of tradition. Why subject young people to *The Idylls of the King* when *John Brown's Body* is available? Why read *Ivanhoe* when *Huckleberry Finn* is just as accessible? The quality of the subject and the style are paramount if we are to develop the discrimination and good taste of our young.

5. *The knowledge or the content is important for adolescents now as well as in the future.* Unless the young person can see some purpose for learning a specific content, or unless he has a need which this knowledge helps to meet, he will learn but little. With the wide variety of possible subjects to read or write or talk about, there is little reason for not suiting the materials to the students.

Subjects for study, however, should have lasting value. There is so much to be learned in the last decades of the twentieth century that no one has time to waste his energies in learning the ephemeral or the inconsequential. Young people enjoy being challenged and they should be, frequently, by subject matter of real interest and consequence.

Broadening and deepening the interests of adolescents are important tasks for the English teacher. This can be done through books which are written in such a manner as to appeal to young people, or through oral sharing of an enthusiasm for some special interest. Occasionally offering a young person a new experience or enticing him into new fields through devious methods will open vistas for him he would otherwise never have seen.

When these guidelines are followed in selecting content for English courses, students generally become enthusiastic participators, and a few may even become scholars.

CHAPTER II

The "How" of English

The purpose for which we perform or learn given tasks has considerable effect on the quality of our performance. If, for instance, the task is to learn when and how to use quotation marks, there are several approaches to gaining this information. If the teacher and the students are concerned chiefly with memorizing the rules for quotation marks as printed in a language textbook and then applying them to sentences in that textbook for the purpose of receiving a satisfactory grade on the next exam, what is learned are the rules and their application according to one authority. On the other hand, if the teacher and the students are concerned about punctuating original short stories or research reports containing direct quotations, they will use the language books and the English handbooks as resources for determining the correct use of quotation marks. Thus the use of resource materials and something about the use of quotation marks are learned as well.

If one is concerned only with rules of punctuation, the former method is more economical. If the concern is for applying punctuation to personal writing, then the more direct method is better. Both methods will produce some knowledge of the use of quotation marks, but what is considered the most important purpose for this knowledge will determine the "how."

The way in which the English curriculum is organized will depend upon what the school system or the teacher believes to be most important in the education of young people. Three factors are always present in any curriculum: the subject matter as an organized discipline; the individual learner; and the society in which the individual learns.

The content may be formal or informal, trivial or of great significance to society—but subject matter there must be. The individual is the only human entity which can be taught. The individual may be grouped with others much like himself, a situation we call *a group* or *a class*. We frequently refer to the group or class as an entity which learns well or poorly, as the case may be. What we mean is that the individuals in the group or class have learned well or poorly, not the group itself. The reaction of individuals to certain learning situations will have considerable effect on what is learned, as any classroom teacher knows.

Individual human beings live in groups; put together in rather close proximity they become a society. Each society has certain characteristics, certain behavior patterns, certain expectations from its members. A public school is an institution belonging to the people, the society; thus, what the society is, wants, and expects from its schools has tremendous influence on the curriculum as well as on the individuals growing up in that society.

Several types of curricular patterns in English instruction have been developed in American public schools: the basic-skills approach, the functional approach, the thematic-units approach, and the literature or readings approach. All these approaches include the three above-mentioned factors. However, each approach is predicated on the premise that one of these factors will be dominant.

Basic Skills Approach

The oldest format and probably the one that is still used most widely in the United States is the study of the elements of English, including the analysis of literature. This is a subject-centered curriculum with the influence of society operating to a degree and with a minimal regard to individual differences.

English as a subject discipline has been analyzed and broken down into its most logical component parts. These elements, in turn, have been examined to determine where and when they can best be taught and learned by children and young people. Uniform agreement among educators has never been reached as to what concepts and skills should be taught when and to whom. Little research has been done in this area. Most decisions as to content have been made on the basis of observation and experience as to what is possible at each grade level. Traditional ways of handling various facets of English have been established. These, in turn, have been reinforced by textbook writers and publishers.

The most common divisions of English as a discipline are the grammar or structure of the English language, the mechanics of

composition (such as punctuation and capitalization), the funda-
mentals of composition (both oral and written), spelling, reading
as a skill, and literature. There are three patterns of organization
which prevail. One is the daily designation of the kind of subject
matter—for instance Monday for spelling, Tuesday for writing,
Wednesday for mechanics, Thursday for reading skills, and Friday
for literature. This plan guarantees coverage of phases of English,
yet gives variety to the weekly schedule. The principal drawback is
that there is little continuity of learning. The lessons must be
planned to complete that day's work without leaving loose ends,
otherwise the balance may be disturbed. For example, if the class
were habitually slow in the reading and discussion or in other work
on a piece of literature and the assignment went over into Monday's
class period, the spelling lesson—or whatever was designated—
would have to be curtailed or skipped altogether. Another disad-
vantage is that when subject matter is divided into such small segments, it is difficult to help the learners see the bigger picture of
the interrelatedness of aspects of language which closer continuity
brings.

The second pattern is the block-of-work plan, sometimes errone-
ously called units of work. Under this arrangement, the various
subject materials to be covered for the year are examined and
divided into logical segments. A tentative fifteen-week schedule
might look something like this:

Ninth-grade English
Study of verb	1 week
Study of the short story	3 weeks
Spelling and vocabulary study	3 days
Study of the use of the colon	2 days
Composition writing	3 days
Book reports	2 days
Study of biography	3 weeks
Composition writing	3 days
Spelling and vocabulary study	2 days
Reading-skill-building—skimming for specific information	2 days
Study of subordinating conjunctions	3 days
Study of the use of the comma	1 week
Study of the informal essay	3 weeks

The subject matter is blocked out in such a manner as to give
balance and variety to the year's work. At the same time, the continuity of ideas can be more readily built. In both this plan and the

one described earlier, the various aspects can be related if the teacher so desires. The composition may serve as the springboard for the study of grammar or punctuation or both. Literature and composition may be correlated to an extent. The principal weakness of the block-of-work organization is that correlation of learning materials is difficult, and many teachers either do not know how to do it or find that it takes considerable effort. As a consequence, punctuation is too frequently taught without relation to composition, or composition without relation to literature, and so on.

The third traditional pattern of organization of English subject matter is the division of content into a semester of literature and a semester of composition and grammar. In this arrangement the literature is usually taught by literary types or in chronological order. The composition and grammar are usually interspersed in the other semester. No reading, except for an occasional book report, is done except in the semester devoted to literature. This plan has been popular in many city school systems. Mid-year promotions are common, and this facilitates the system. A student who fails has to repeat only a half-year rather than a whole year. Transfer from one school to another is easier because the person who moves is less likely to miss an important work segment or to have to repeat material he has just gone over. What element is to be studied, and when, is more exactly determined under this plan.

On the other hand, the drawbacks of this plan are also numerous. First, there is more rigidity in the program for both teacher and student. Correlation of literature and composition is apt to be limited. Although some writing may be done in relation to the literature, the bulk of the composition work proceeds without reference to what has been read.

Authorities in the field of English education generally frown on the semester plan. The National Council of Teachers of English official publication on the secondary school English curriculum is quite explicit in its statement:

> . . . The language arts are closely interrelated. The day is past when English programs were organized with one term of writing, one term of literature, and one term of speech. The sequential program for all students utilizes all the language arts in every term.[1]

---

[1] Commission on the English Curriculum of The National Council of Teachers of English, *The English Language Arts in the Secondary School* (New York: Appleton-Century-Crofts, Inc., © 1956), p. 68. Reprinted by permission of Appleton-Century-Crofts.

Much stress is placed on the interrelatedness of the aspects of language. Effective speakers can be evaluated only by effective listeners. Good writers must have perceptive readers in order to accomplish their purposes. The semester plan appears to be on its way out although it still has many strongholds in American schools.

A fourth type of subject-centered organization is not traditional but is gaining approval from some of the more conservative leaders in English education. This might be called the readings plan, or the literature → composition → structure pattern. The arrows between the parts indicate a sequential linkage. Appropriate pieces of literature are selected to be read by the class. These would include considerable amounts of informal essays as well as novels, short stories, plays, poems, and biographies. The basis for study is the literary selection or group of selections. Discussion of the material in terms of some analysis of its structure, its meaning, and the literary devices used by the author occurs both before and after most of the reading. Other oral techniques may be used, such as dramatization or role-playing. Writing about the selection follows. Composition techniques and skills are taught as the student progresses from one level to the next. The literature furnishes the basic material around which the composition is written. Very little imaginative writing is done. The mechanics and grammar are taught through analysis of the compositions, the chief aim being to improve writing skills.

The readings plan gives opportunity for correlating all phases of language study. It also gives a concrete basis for composition and thus for language study through the readings. Too frequently young people complain that they have nothing to write about or that the assigned topic is one about which they have no background. This plan eliminates this problem. On the other hand, the readings plan does not allow for imaginative writing, nor does it aid students in solving many of their everyday communication problems.

Several advantages of the subject-centered approach are evident. Students can be exposed to the discipline of English in an organized, sequential fashion. This insures the coverage of the material considered most important. If the field of English is as important as most educators and citizens believe, then it is well to have assurance that all its aspects are taught.

The disadvantages are also evident. The course planning for each grade level is frequently done by a committee of teachers teaching at that level or by each teacher for himself. In cases like these, there is seldom any planning among various grade levels. Consequently, there is apt to be much wasteful repetition of some phases and some important omissions in others. This is not inevitable, of course, but it does occur often.

Motivation is often a problem in the subject-centered English curriculum. Young people live very much in the present. Most regard a thirty-year-old as too old to "know the score." Too frequently they have no more purpose in life than thrills and excitement. Identifying parts of speech, writing reports on authors' lives, or even writing letters are all learning activities for which many can see little use. They have no immediate need for these skills or this kind of information, and deferred values hold little allure for most adolescents.

Some of these youths are discouraged learners, especially in English. Time after time they have written compositions only to have them so red-penciled that they did not know where to begin to improve them. Their reading skills are also usually very poor. Teachers in the past may have tried to help them overcome their difficulties, but all too often such efforts have not been very productive. These discouraged learners drop farther and farther behind until they feel the whole business of education in general and English in particular is futile and thus a waste of time. There is little in the subject-centered approach which can be used to appeal to these young people to try again.

Then there are the reluctant learners—perhaps able enough academically, but with attention focused upon the here and now to the exclusion of the past and future. Unless coercion is used (and even that does not always work) most reluctant learners can be reached only through an appeal to their immediate needs. This is not impossible in a subject-centered approach, but it takes a teacher who has imagination and who thoroughly understands young people to make it work.

Functional Approach

Functional learning is frequently equated with utility. Can the information or skill be put to some constructive use by the learner in his society? This is the paramount question in determining the content and structure of the functional curriculum. The nature of the society and its expectations for its members determine, in large part, what is most useful to the learner. Classical Greek or Hebrew would have very little utility for an Eskimo who expects to remain in the frozen North the rest of his life. On the other hand, young men studying for the priesthood or the ministry are likely to find a knowledge of Greek and Hebrew an important tool in unlocking the mysteries of Biblical passages.

During the late 1920's, the 1930's, and the early part of the 1940's, many authorities in English education were advocating the functional concept of the curriculum. Wilbur Hatfield, long-time executive secretary of the National Council of Teachers of English, was chairman of a curriculum commission of the National Council charged with responsibility for developing a curriculum pattern for English, Grades K–12. The result was a guide based upon the functional, or experience approach, and was published in 1935.

In setting the basic principles for this curriculum pattern, the commission urged English teachers to make use of the formal and informal cocurricular activities of the school as well as situations in the community:

> The pupils of the elementary and high school are also frequently engaged in personal and community enterprises which involve them in language situations. If the English teacher can contrive means of "following" them out into these situations and connecting up the school work in English with the actual scenes in which English is employed, she will widen her classroom to community dimensions.[2]

The guide further attempted to show teachers how to make English meaningful (and thus useful) to students through practical, everyday experiences such as discussing movies, learning to follow directions from road guides or recipes, or practicing informal conversation in a group.

Surveys were made of the ways in which people actually used language. Spelling needs were ascertained by examining hundreds of words written and read by all sorts of children and young people. Standard lists were compiled to be used as a basis for writing spelling texts. Among the better-known word lists were those compiled by Thorndike, Horn, Dolch, Rinsland, and Fitzgerald.

---

[2] W. Wilbur Hatfield, Chairman, *An Experience Curriculum in English:* A Report of the Curriculum Commission of The National Council of Teachers of English (New York: Appleton-Century-Crofts, Inc., 1935), p. 6.

As a result of this research, several important discoveries about spelling were made. One startling finding was that 90 per cent of the words in people's writing fell within the first one thousand words in frequency of use as determined through a study of adult writing.[3] In general these are the common, everyday words, which have among them what language books call "spelling demons"—*their* and *there, its* and *it's, surprise, library,* and *sincerely,* for example. This kind of information has led to greater stress on learning to spell words needed by children and young people in their writing and less on those that were unusual and little-known.

Research was done on the relative importance of the various aspects of language in daily life. It was discovered that 42 per cent of the average person's time is spent listening; speaking is a close second, followed by reading and, last, writing. The conclusion of the curriculum-makers was that at least some time should be spent on the skills of listening in the English class and that there should be more speaking than writing because of the greater need for the former skill.

Julias Boraas investigated the correlation between knowledge of formal grammar and practical mastery of English.

He found that such knowledge correlated *highest with ability in arithmetic, and least of all* (.28) *with ability in composition,* the very skill with which grammar, to be of value, should show a significant relationship. Similar findings were reported by Catherine Catherwood for schools in Minnesota and by Mabel C. Benfer for schools in Iowa.[4]

These findings and other similar ones did much to put grammar in disrepute with many teachers. They began to experiment with the teaching of the mechanics and skills of writing without benefit of much formal grammar on the part of students. This procedure appeared to many teachers—and this has been borne out by research —to produce as good, if not better, results than the formal instruction of grammar. Strom, in her summary of the research on grammar and usage and its implications for teaching writing, says:

---

[3] The Casis School Faculty, *Spelling Instruction: A Curriculum-Wide Approach,* directed and edited by Thomas D. Horn and Henry J. Otto (Austin: The University of Texas, 1954), p. 14.
[4] John J. DeBoer, Walter V. Kaulfers, and Helen Rand Miller, *Teaching Secondary English* (New York: McGraw-Hill Book Company, Inc., 1951), p. 59.

The research findings show clearly and overwhelmingly that direct methods of instruction, focusing on writing activities and the structuring of ideas, are more efficient in teaching sentence structure, usage, punctuation, and other related factors than are such methods as nomenclature drill, diagramming, and rote memorization of grammatical rules.[5]

Other surveys showed the kinds of language situations which young people and adults use most frequently. As a result, lessons based on these findings were constructed on using the telephone, making introductions, making announcements, reading newspapers and magazines, listening to the radio, conversing with friends, leading a discussion, making written or oral reports on topics of interest or concern, note-taking and outlining, reading books of interest, and similar subjects as suggested in *An Experience Curriculum in English.*

About this same time many educators were becoming aware of the needs in American society. If democracy was to flourish, if a better standard of living for all people was to become a reality, if every child and adult was to have an opportunity to develop himself to his fullest capacities, education would have to be organized with these ends in mind. Vocational needs became more important; community improvement through cooperative efforts became a reality in many places; thus the needs and concerns of society became important factors in the public school curriculum.

The tone of this discussion on the functional curriculum may have left the erroneous impression that organizing a curriculum of a school around the needs of society is a thing of the past. It is true that this concept had its largest group of followers among school people during the 1930's and early 1940's, and some exciting experiments in community school operation and the experience curriculum were carried on during that time. Remnants of this movement can still be seen in many high schools which have excellent programs of distributive education, or where school service clubs undertake to work with community agencies for civic improvement. In the last several years there has also been a revival of the school-community idea in sections of the Middle West. With the present concern for school dropouts it is conceivable that curricu-

---

[5] Ingrid M. Strom, *Research in Grammar and Usage and Its Implications for Teaching Writing,* Bulletin of the School of Education, Indiana University, III, 5 (September 1960), 13–14.

lums for such groups and perhaps others may be developed around this concept.

The influence of this functional concept of learning can be seen readily in language books even today. These books are often organized around a number of everyday language situations such as "Making the Report," "Reading the Newspaper," or "Using the Dictionary." There is an attempt to make the mechanics of composition—such as using commas or developing variety in sentence structure—meaningful to young people. Many of the authors of these textbooks have put great effort into making the exercises interesting and purposeful. This was not generally true of earlier editions of these texts or of similar ones published thirty years ago.

The concept of extensive reading of books of the students' own choice was a result of the change of emphasis in education from that of learning a body of knowledge to that of learning what was useful and of concern to the individual and his society. Under the functional approach, the content of literature study in the secondary school no longer consisted of a series of traditional selections to be read by everyone at a given grade level; rather, it consisted of a wide variety of selections chosen for their appeal to young people and read according to individual tastes and needs. (See also Chapters IV and V.)

The functional approach encourages correlation of English with other subjects. The English teacher works with the science teacher in planning the teaching of how to report facts objectively and draw reasonable generalizations or conclusions. Or the English teacher works with the American history teacher in planning the reading of American literature of a given period or on a certain fact or concept of a period to coincide with the study of the history of that period or concept. Papers on particular aspects of American life could be written for both classes, with the English teacher marking the paper for structure, organization, and mechanics, and the history teacher reacting more specifically to the ideas the paper contains.

Fusion of the contents of English and social studies at the junior high school level is still quite prevalent throughout the country. In this arrangement one teacher teaches both English and the social studies to the same group of students. In this arrangement, the language skills are taught mainly in relation to the social studies material: vocabulary is built around the subject under discussion;

reporting techniques are studied and evaluated through the need to report certain kinds of information from the social studies; reading skills, such as skimming and drawing inferences, are taught through searching for a specific name or date and studying a political speech for innuendoes. In these fused programs there may be some English for its own sake, but most of the work is done in relation to the social studies content.

Advocates of the fused Social Studies–English program believe that you cannot talk talking nor write writing. You must have something to talk or write about. Because social studies content depends so much on reading, writing, listening, and speaking, it is economical of learning time and effort to link social studies with English. There is much useful purpose in learning language skills when they are related to purposeful learning and activities in another area. Frequently, for instance, the learning of spelling or of outlining appears more efficient when the young person has some practical use for the knowledge, as in writing a report on "Recreational Opportunities for Young People in Centerville." Another advantage of the fused program may be that the teacher who teaches the language skills as well as the social studies will insist that skills are to be learned and used for more than just passing tests and getting satisfactory grades. There is evidence that accuracy and effectiveness in writing and speaking are developed best through the student's working on the "what" and the "how" of the material as a unit. In this way an understanding is built that content and structure are integral parts of the whole when communication is involved.

Most of the advantages of the functional approach have been presented in the foregoing discussion. They may be summarized as follows:

1. Useful knowledge of immediate concern is more readily learned than information or skills for which the young person has no immediate use.

2. Functional learning can lead the way to cooperative problem-solving, which is a part of democratic procedure. In a democratic society the tenets of democracy must be practiced, as well as taught, in the schools.

3. The functional approach attempts to make English useful to all young people, to stress those language and literature skills and knowledges which are commonly used in our society, and to elim-

inate many of those things which are often learned for learning's sake or because of tradition. For many people much of the formal, organized knowledge in any academic field appears to be of little personal value unless it serves as a basis for a special interest or vocational choice.

4. More flexibility is generally allowed in the functional approach to curriculum than in the subject-centered approach. There is not the pressure of being sure that everything has been taught regardless of the needs of the learner in ability and interest. The functional approach allows wide latitude in what is taught and how it is taught. The guiding principles are: Is the material or skill useful in this society now and is it apt to be in the future? Is it in accord with the ideals and tenets of our society?

5. The functional approach serves to reinforce learning through making application in more than one subject field as in correlation or fusion of English with other subjects.

6. The functional approach tends to demonstrate the interrelatedness of knowledge and learning.

7. The functional approach furnishes a constructive means of providing or selecting content with which to teach all of the aspects of English.

Weaknesses in the functional approach are also evident. Probably its greatest drawback is also its greatest strength—judging worth of learning by its utility. Slow and meager progress could be made in any of the areas of modern life if there were not people curious enough to delve into and ferret out knowledge for knowledge's sake.

Hundreds of men and women find deep satisfaction and true enjoyment from the pursuit of knowledge for its own sake. For the true scholar—and there are many such both young and old—the sense of discovery is sufficient reward for great amounts of effort in the search for answers to questions and problems yet unsolved.

The taste for scholarship often develops early. If the insatiable curiosity which young children have about their world and everything concerning it can be kept alive into adolescence, they will acquire much knowledge enthusiastically and voluntarily. Many children are curious about words—not only what they mean and how they are used, but also how they originated and how they have changed. Other young people become fascinated by the dialects and sound variations in their language, and this can lead to a fruitful study of linguistics through dialects. Still other young scholars become interested in what and how people wrote in the past or what recognized authors and poets have had to say about various subjects —such as death, freedom, man's destiny, or war and peace, to name only a few. This kind of interest can be cultivated by enthusiastic, knowledgeable teachers using curriculum patterns and materials which challenge and stimulate the young person to learn and discover new ideas and relationships in the many areas of language study.

We greatly limit the areas of learning in the secondary school if we insist that all knowledge must have immediate as well as future utility. Limitations on knowledge can be harmful both to the individual and to the society. The modern world cries for more knowledge, not less. The young people in our schools today will live in an expanding future. No one knows for sure what will be utilitarian by 1999.

In some cases, conformity may be the result of the functional approach. The status quo may be the norm by which utility is determined. When this happens, there is little challenge to evaluate the present mode of usage against that of another time or place. Writing is taught as though there were only a few set patterns of organization of a composition. Little allowance is made for an individual approach to a problem in the theme. Students read only that material which they value. Slight attention is given to the aesthetic values of literature. The functional approach does not necessarily impose conformity on the learners, but this may happen when the approach is used by teachers who do not really understand the theory behind it.

On the other hand, the functional approach has contributed much to making learning meaningful and purposeful for more students. It has shown us the desirability of relating various areas of subject matter to each other in such a way as to reinforce the learning which is of real importance to young people and society.

Thematic Unit Approach

As more and more has been learned about the adolescent and his characteristics through careful observation and research, the importance of motivating adolescents toward positive learning goals in all areas of life has become abundantly clear. Research has shown time and time again that human beings learn most efficiently (in terms of effort and powers of retention) when the individual learner accepts the purposes of learning as his own. Acceptance of these purposes implies commitment to them.

How to obtain that commitment on the part of young people is a major concern of educators. Studies show that the interests of young people are developmental in nature. Seventh- and eighth-graders are generally interested in animals, sports, pioneers, cowboys and Western life, young love, and so forth. Ninth- and tenth-graders are more interested in detective stories, travel, manners and personality, dating and family problems, and historical fiction. The interests of eleventh- and twelfth-graders are closer to those of adults. Special, individual interests—science, music, poetry, drama, sports cars, and fashion design, to mention only a few—are often followed with much depth as well as enthusiasm. Vocational choice, plans for marriage and family, concerns about the state of the world, and efforts to evolve a satisfactory personal philosophy of life are common problems of these more mature adolescents.

Because young people, as well as everyone else, are motivated to learn best through their own interests and concerns, many curriculum-makers began to explore the possibility of capitalizing on these interests. Thematic units developed, based upon the findings of numerous studies on the interests of adolescents. The English curriculum seemed to be particularly adaptable to this approach. Language and its use is a personal matter. Each of us needs to learn how to glean information we want from the written word or from listening to other people. We also need to learn how to express what we know, feel, and believe in such a way that others can understand what we are really trying to say. But before we can do this we must have information, be aroused to express emotion, and formulate basic convictions—in other words, have something to say. Our interests furnish us with the motivation to communicate.

The influence of the thematic-unit approach has been evident in the literature and reading textbooks published since 1940. It is not uncommon to find the literature for a particular grade level grouped under themes such as "Tone: The Lighter Touch," "Theme: The Right Decision," "Point of View: Through the Eyes of Youth," "Plot: Dramatic Action," "Character: Memorable People," "Not

Exactly Serious," "Poems with a Touch of a Shiver," "Freedom's Ferment," "Six Comments on Love," and others which are listed in the latest edition for tenth grade of a popular literature series.[6] Literature texts above and below tenth grade follow the same general pattern. Many times a teacher feels that the selections must have been chosen for the text before the themes were decided upon, for the selections do not always seem appropriate to the theme under which they are classified. In other words, some textbooks give the appearance of being thematically oriented when in reality they would make good materials for out-and-out subject-centered English curriculums if organized under more traditional headings. But for all this, the selections are generally better suited to adolescent interests than formerly.

Evidence of the popularity of the thematic-unit approach is seen in the English curriculum guides of such states as Florida and Minnesota, or of such cities as Denver and San Francisco, and in small school districts such as Katy or Andrews, Texas.

The first volume of the report of the Commission on the English Curriculum (published in 1952) recommends strongly and unequivocally that the unit method is the best organization for the English curriculum.[7] In speaking of the junior high school program, this group said:

> A sufficiently broad program of units in the junior high school will inevitably require experience with all aspects and many processes of language, at levels appropriate to boys and girls of this age.[8]

In the discussion of the senior high school program, they say:

> The kind of program described for junior high school is being developed also as the most adequate for the senior high. Broad areas of need, experience, and interest are selected as centers around which study, investigation and inquiry, experience and experiment are conducted.[9]

The third curriculum volume, *The English Language Arts in the*

---

[6] Walter Loban, Dorothy Holmstrom, and Luella B. Cook, *Adventures in Appreciation* (New York: Harcourt, Brace & World, Inc., 1958), pp. v–ix.

[7] Commission on the English Curriculum of The National Council of Teachers of English, *The English Language Arts* (New York: Appleton-Century-Crofts, Inc., © 1952), pp. 111–17. Reprinted by permission of Appleton-Century-Crofts.

[8] *Ibid.*, p. 116.

[9] *Ibid.*, p. 130.

Secondary School (published in 1956) gives detailed suggestions as to how to organize a thematic unit and how to teach it.

The thematic-unit approach has strengths and weaknesses, as do other plans. Many of these may be evident in the foregoing discussion. Specifically, the strengths can be stated as follows:

1. Motivation for learning English is greatly enhanced by this method of organization. The fact that the material to be learned is based upon adolescent interests and concerns makes it much more appealing to young people: they can identify with the subject material more easily. Learning is more efficient if the learner *wants* to know about what he is to learn. He also will probably retain what he learns longer because it has real meaning for him. The skills he develops are tools which have a function. A young person is much more likely to remember that a colon is generally used after the salutation in a formal business or personal letter, for example, if he actually writes a letter to a business or professional man asking permission to visit his place of business on a field trip. The motivations for learning are more directly tied to what is learned than to the grade received, as in the subject-centered approach, for instance.

2. Language is a composite of many skills and knowledges which must be related for effective learning. The thematic-unit approach is a natural vehicle for relating all language aspects. Discussion follows reading and usually precedes writing, and listening is a part of discussion. When a theme such as "Finding One's Way into the World of Work" is used, it is comparatively simple to see how a lively discussion would follow the reading of "Quality" by John Galsworthy and that, as a result of this discussion, the class might be asked to write on the topic, "Quality of Work Versus Getting the Job Done." An analysis of errors in punctuation and sentence structure would follow, with perhaps some concentrated study of parallel construction or devices for contrast.

3. Continuity in approach and learning can be fostered. English teachers and curriculum-coordinators must plan to insure proper placement of themes for a developmental sequence for Grades 7–12. Similarly, continuity of content must be planned to be certain that language skills and knowledges will be assigned to the proper developmental level.

4. Through the use of a variety of materials and methods, more individual students are likely to be served. For example, if the

theme "Animals in Our World" were used in the seventh grade, some children with reading disabilities might thoroughly enjoy some of Thornton Burgess' "Mother West Wind Stories," which are easy reading, yet have enough interest to hold the attention of a young adolescent (if his enjoyment of fancy has not been spoiled by the pseudosophistication of adult television shows). Other young adolescents might enjoy Ditmar's account of how, as a boy, he became interested in snakes. Still others might respond more positively to Rawlings' *The Yearling,* or Eric Knight's *Lassie Come Home,* or Gipson's *Old Yeller.* There is an abundance of material for such a theme, and every young person should find something he can understand which also challenges him.

The wide scope of materials from which to choose makes possible individualization of assignments through group work or individual projects. This allows the weak or immature student to succeed and, at the same time, pushes the able student to higher levels of attainment.

5. Although the primary function of the American public school is to develop academic skills and knowledge, a close second function is to assist children and young people to become positive contributors to our culture. This can be done in many ways, of course, but it implies the development of the individual learner in all aspects of life—health, vocation, family relationships—to his fullest potential. Helping adolescents face and solve their problems is essential to their ultimate development toward maturity. The thematic-unit approach deals directly with some of the persistent problem areas of youth— "Knowing My Way Around: Customs and Courtesies," "Ways of Employing Leisure Time," "Making the Most of Oneself," "Finding One's Way into the World of Work," or "What Does Literature Have to Tell Me about God?" are a few examples. Reading, writing, and talking about these problems and what other young people like themselves have done to solve them can go far in helping individuals to face and solve their own problems more effectively.

The weaknesses in the thematic-unit approach are also evident. They can be summarized under three categories:

1. When the interests and concerns of young people in our modern world are taken as the basis for themes around which to organize content and method in English, it is difficult to be sure that all the necessary language learnings have been thoroughly taught and as

thoroughly learned. Many other ideas besides those of English are incorporated into a thematic unit. Unless care is taken in planning for the full sequence, there may be gaps in the learnings. If it is left to the individual teacher to plan and execute units without rather specific planning of the over-all program, the result is apt to be an overemphasis on some phases of English and a neglect of others.

2. Although apparently abundant, reading material that bears directly on the theme and at the same time meets the needs of students at various reading levels is often difficult to locate in quantity. Yet without some worthwhile reading material, a unit cannot be effective. True, information can be gleaned from interviews, field trips, films, and so forth; but reading matter provides the bulk of the background, the necessary facts and attitudes, and the illustration through meaningful content of the fact that ideas can be conveyed in print and in various styles.

Too frequently a theme becomes a device around which a number of good but unrelated readings and activities are organized. The theme becomes a smokescreen behind which may be hidden very little that could not be better taught through a direct subject-matter approach. When this occurs, the purposes for using thematic units are obviated and pupils are no more highly motivated by unit teaching of this kind than through the direct subject-matter approach. In fact, the direct approach is likely to have the greater appeal under these circumstances.

3. Although when properly planned and taught, the thematic-unit approach alleviates some of the problems of motivation, this type of organization requires more teaching skill than any other. Almost anyone with a reasonable amount of intelligence and college training in teaching can follow a high school language or literature text. But when content is organized around themes, and activities and assignments are suited to individual needs and differences, teaching becomes a complex operation. The teacher often must help four or five groups, each with a different objective; at the same time he must be sure that opportunities for skill-building are capitalized upon and that the learning each group is engaged in is appropriate to the theme and thus meaningful to the learner. Unit teaching is hard work, although many teachers find it amply rewarding.

Compromises

Although each of the three basic approaches has been presented in a "pure" form, this does not mean that they exist just this way in actual practice. It does mean, however, that even in an eclectic approach one method and philosophy of teaching will predominate.

A subjective but conservative estimate, based on wide experience with the patterns and practices of English teaching in the United States, is that upward of 90 per cent of the content taught in secondary school English classes is organized and approached from some type of subject-centered standpoint. The other 10 per cent, and probably less, will be divided between the thematic approach and the functional approach.

There are many compromise curricular patterns in effect in English classrooms. One of these is the thematic-unit approach interspersed with interludes of functional or subject-centered material. Thus there may be a unit on "Understanding Ourselves and Others," followed by a week or more devoted to the skills involved in expository writing. This, in turn, might be followed by an intensive study of *Julius Caesar* before another thematic unit is taken up.

Under the subject-centered approach, thematic units may be combined with types of literature. For example, a unit on "Many Moods of Love" using poetry might include poems which not only fit the theme but also are examples of good poetry. The figurative language of poetry, the meter and rhyme scheme, the symbols used —all might be studied in some depth. Contrasting ways of expressing one's feelings in poetry can be explored by studying several love poems written by different poets. Thus poetry as such can be combined with the thematic-unit approach. Or a unit might be centered on the problem of differences and likenesses between life in England and in the United States, using novels which effectively depict life in either or both countries. The structure of the novel can be studied at the same time.

Even when an out-and-out subject-centered approach is used, with types of literature or chronology as the center of organization, there is generally some deviation. The themes are used to motivate in some cases. In a chronological organization, correlation with—or at least some attention to—the history of the country and period might be considered functional learning.

A study of how language changes, how usage patterns are established, how dialects enrich and affect the American language is both a functional and a subject-centered unit. An effective study of our language leads beyond the superficial observations based on textbook rules of "correct" or "incorrect" usage. Such a study teaches students how to observe spoken language patterns intelligently, how to discover origins of words and trace their use historically, how to adapt usage to the appropriate style for the time and place. To do all this, many sources of information are used by the students and teacher. Various types of references, such as standard American dictionaries of various periods, studies of American usage by recognized linguistic scholars, samples of writing by recognized authors of various periods, and famous speeches of different historical periods are all used by students under the teacher's guidance. In addition, students will make simple usage studies of their own according to their abilities.

A language emphasis such as that described above permeates a full year of English study in some high schools. Nearly everything that is read, written, spoken, or heard is at some time looked at in relation to what these young people have learned or are learning about language.

Another important emphasis which has developed during the last few years is the close reading of carefully selected pieces of literature. The primary aim is to teach students how to read for meaning. For example, if Hemingway's *The Old Man and the Sea* is the novel being studied, the class is asked to pay special attention to Hemingway's use of symbols in this story. What does the fish represent? How does Hemingway make this clear? Defend your opinion by citing passages from the book. Do you think there is room for disagreement on this point? Defend your position.

These are only sample questions which might be asked about the novel for the purpose of helping young people to read accurately for meaning. In order to understand some authors or some passages, sentence structure may need to be analyzed from the standpoint of word order, modification, or special word meanings. Thus language structure becomes an integral part of the study. Some time during such a study, there will be a need to interpret, through well-organized writing assignments, ideas associated with the reading. At this time composition problems are studied and worked on. In this way all aspects of language learning can be fused with the intensive study of a piece of literature.

No "best" curricular organization for secondary English exists, apart from the philosophy of education held by the curriculum-makers and by the teachers who put it into operation. Strengths and weaknesses can be found in any relatively consistent pattern. The real question to be asked before curriculum work begins is: What do we, as the English faculty of this secondary school, believe to be of primary importance for our students? In a good school, the answer to this question will reiterate and supplement the philosophy of the whole school.

CHAPTER III

The "Who" of English

One of the outstanding characteristics of the American secondary schools is the provision for all the children in the society. Although there are many strengths in this arrangement, problems also readily occur. A wide range of intellectual capacity as well as a wide variety of talents and abilities are found among students in every American high school.

The differences among students in the ability to handle the various factors of English are just as great. One student may read efficiently and widely, but be unable to express his ideas on paper. Another may enjoy the study of the mechanics and structure of language while detesting all literature. One seventh-grader may read as well as a high school senior while another high school senior may read only as well as an average seventh-grader. These problems are real and must be faced by every teacher of high school English.

Several plans for solution of the problem have been developed over the years. For example, the Dalton and the Winnetka Plans were each devised to meet individual differences through a shift in class organization and scheduling. Although neither plan may have been completely practical, the main reason for their not being tried very extensively was that they did away with the conventional classroom organization, a time-honored tradition in American secondary schools.

Within the last five years there has been extensive experimentation with flexible scheduling in a few large high schools. Many variations have been tried—some classes may meet every day while others meet only two or three times a week; some periods may be only thirty minutes long (for such purposes as spelling drills) while others may extend for over an hour to provide sufficient time for field trips, firsthand research, and experimentation. Usually in schools in which flexible scheduling is attempted, some kind of independent study is offered the more able and more highly motivated students in selected subjects. Students are assigned to courses not only on the basis of the number of years they have been in school but also in accordance with their academic potential and interest. This type of scheduling attempts to provide a flexible curriculum for a variety of students with varying abilities, needs, and interests.

A possible pattern for English in one of these schools experimenting with a flexible schedule might include sixty-minute classes three or four times a week for study of the different types of literature, some intensive reading of a few carefully selected works, study of the history and structure of the language, and work in various types of written and oral composition. Several thirty-minute periods each week might be scheduled for students on the basis of need in spelling, mechanics of composition, usage, guidance in recreational reading, or improvement of reading skills. In addition, a strong remedial program providing more short periods of intensive practice in skills with no more than three one-hour periods per week in classes working with more structured literary content and writing problems might be available for those less able in English. These would be assigned to a teacher who acts as coordinator and English counselor, assigning and adjusting specific schedules. A similar kind of special program might be made available for the academically able students in English, substituting longer periods of independent study for the short drill periods but with much emphasis on the needs and potentials of the individual student.

This kind of program requires highly skilled teachers who are able to assess the materials to meet these needs. Much teamwork is required, as well as the ability to adapt oneself to various schedules and patterns of teaching. Schools operating effectively with flexible schedules and curriculum patterns are not likely to become numerous in the immediate future. As yet there are too many problems involved for most administrators and faculties to undertake the changes. Perhaps in the future—if and when high school counselors are sufficiently numerous and well trained to assume the burden of academic diagnosis, English teachers (and teachers in other areas) are educated to adapt the curriculum to meet various intellectual needs and abilities, and administrators are adept at manipulating time and space in such a way that schedules are adapted to curricular needs and not vice versa—secondary schools with flexible curriculums and schedules may become the rule rather than the exception. In the meantime, this kind of school can serve as a goal and other kinds of lesser adaptations to individual differences will help alleviate the problem as well as make better use of school personnel.[1]

Grouping

The educational literature has been full of the pros and cons of grouping students into heterogeneous or homogeneous classes for teaching and learning. *Heterogeneity,* in this discussion, will mean the grouping of students into classes according to the number of years they have attended school and their chronological age. Individual or specific levels of intelligence or achievement are not considered, but each class would have a wide range of abilities and drive among its members.

Homogeneity refers to the practice of separating the students of a given grade level according to standardized test scores, previous grades in the subject, IQ, and counselor opinion. The objective is to group those students who are most alike in academic ability and achievement.

The theory behind homogeneous grouping holds that when there is less difference in academic achievement in a given class, the task of teaching becomes easier and more effective. A range of scores representing an eight-year spread in reading achievement in a heterogeneous ninth- or tenth-grade English class is not unusual. If this range can be reduced to two or even three years in a single class group, many teachers believe they will be able to provide a more realistic learning situation for students. Reading materials can be provided more readily from a fifth- to an eighth-grade level than they can from a fifth- to a twelfth-grade level. Similarly, teachers can more easily adjust content to the needs of a group with a smaller range of abilities. Grouping according to achievement and ability can be advantageous to all levels of learners. The less able learner is given additional help and encouragement as well as materials to assist him to gain the basic reading, writing, and speaking skills he needs for everyday living. He also has the opportunity to succeed in his learning in such a class, for the material is within his ability range and the learning pace is one he can maintain. The very able student likewise has the opportunity of being challenged by content

---

[1] "Locus of Change: Staff Utilization Studies," *The Bulletin of the National Association of the Secondary-School Principals,* XLVI, 270 (January 1962).

which will stimulate him. He will not be held back by those who do not have the background or the capacity to learn on a more abstract verbal level.

Strong arguments against ability grouping can also be found. Unfortunately, although the theory behind grouping implies a differentiated curriculum for the various learning levels, there is actually little difference in content at the different levels. The same basic content is given to all learners of a particular grade level. Inadequate provision of teaching materials is one cause of this: seldom does a school system provide a wide enough range in levels of text materials for any grade level. Generally, one basic textbook is provided together with a few supplementary books for special purposes. If homogeneous grouping is to meet the needs of the various designated levels, then suitable learning materials for each level must be provided. The content to be learned must also be varied to suit the level of the learners.

Unfortunately, there is not perfect correlation among the various aspects of language skills within a given person. Some people use the spoken word quite adequately but write very poorly; others may write quite ably but have low reading ability. How are such individuals to be grouped into homogeneous classes? The average language-achievement score may be a relatively poor index of the particular abilities or needs of a given individual.

Strong arguments are also presented for heterogeneous grouping. In a democratic society, where individuals will be thrown together to make community decisions and to vote, it may be well to be sure that they have learned to communicate with one another and to respect one another in school. In the heterogeneously grouped class, one may find the executive's son asking help on a writing assignment from a plumber's son; or the young people who come from well-to-do homes may suddenly understand the problems of a favorite classmate who cannot afford a new formal for the prom.

Young people may learn as much from one another as they do from the teacher. A class discussion on the kind of person Emily is, as revealed by what others said about her in Thornton Wilder's *Our Town,* can bring out personal views of individuals in the group. Their attitudes, their ways of looking at people, their understanding of their own motives and of the motives of others may be challenged by their peers. It is not uncommon in a lively class discussion to hear a low achiever reveal some understandings about other people that the brighter or more academically able may not have experienced. Usually in a heterogeneous class there are three or four verbally able persons who have ideas which may spark the rest of the group. Without this nucleus to help him, the English teacher is all too frequently delivering a monologue. If diversity of thinking is a desirable trait to encourage, then the more opportunities there are for students to share ideas with others who have a wide range of backgrounds and abilities, the broader and deeper will their learnings be.

Achievement grouping does not alleviate all the ills of the classroom. Some experts feel that, because there is a range and variety of learning levels in even the most closely grouped class, a somewhat wider range does not increase the problems much but forces the teacher to look at his students as individuals with very different learning needs. The teacher of the homogeneously grouped class may be lulled into a false security, thinking all his students are alike when it comes to learning while they may actually be markedly different. Lou La Brant adds another dimension to the weaknesses in ability grouping:

> The brilliant student has taken from him the most difficult language problem he can face: the problem of making himself clear to those with less ability than he. . . . Today the gap between the average or less-than-average man and the highly trained scientist is so great that our scientists are desperate about their ability to explain what they know about their discoveries and inventions.[2]

Teaching the Low Achiever

Despite all of the weaknesses of the plan of grouping students by ability and achievement, many secondary schools are using it. Since World War II—and particularly since 1958, when the "war babies" first hit the seventh grade—the trend has been to increase grouping. Various plans have been used. Conant, in his report on the status of the American high school, recommended that three groupings be made:

> In the required subjects and those elected by a wide range of ability, the students should be grouped according to ability, subject by subject. For example, in English, American history, ninth-grade

---

[2] Lou La Brant, *We Teach English* (New York: Harcourt, Brace & World, Inc., 1951), p. 241.

algebra, biology, and physical science, there should be at least three types of classes—one for the more able in the subject, another for the large group whose ability is above average, and another for the very slow readers who should be handled by special teachers. The middle group might be divided into two or three sections according to the students' abilities in the subject in question. . . . Under the scheme here recommended, for example, a student may be in the top section in English but the middle section in history or ninth-grade algebra.[3]

However, he warned that if the American comprehensive high school is to continue to flourish there must be some classes, notably the homeroom and twelfth-grade social studies class, where there is no division by achievement level. This fraternization with all types of young people will build understanding and appreciation for one another, Conant thinks.

In many schools the bottom 10 per cent (approximately) of those enrolled have long been put into separate groups. These have been known in the local school system variously as remedial or "R" classes, as "special" classes, as "X" classes, or by any designation the school administration thinks appropriate. Frequently, English classes of this kind were assigned to teachers who had some training or experience in teaching reading. Sometimes the principal assigned these classes to the less popular teachers or to the newest teachers on the faculty. Many administrators justified this procedure by saying that probably most of these young people would never finish high school, and that if they had not learned enough in the first six years of school, they probably would not learn in high school—so why waste good teachers on them? Besides, simply clearing other classes of these "hopelessly" retarded ones would facilitate learning for the rest. Needless to say, many teachers shunned teaching these classes whenever possible.

When teachers have been prepared both professionally and emotionally for teaching slow learners, marked progress often results. Retarded adolescents have become less defensive and have experienced new hope for themselves because a teacher was truly interested in helping them. More recently, the general practice is to distribute such classes among all members of the English faculty, each one taking his turn. In a relatively few secondary schools

---

[3] James Bryant Conant, *The American High School Today* (New York: Mc-Graw-Hill Book Company, Inc., 1959), p. 49.

special courses of study have been worked out by teachers who have had previous experience teaching the less able students.[4] Once the course of study is put into use, many teaching-learning materials on a low-reading, high-interest level are necessary for success with these frustrated and too often disillusioned young people. Little research has been done to determine the effectiveness of such specially planned courses on the learners. Such research is badly needed.

Teaching machines. There is some evidence that the teaching machine may be a godsend to the teacher of low-level English classes. Slow learners generally need to have the learning material broken down into simple steps, with each step repeated many times. Repetition is time-consuming for the teacher and often frustrating. A machine never loses patience: it will repeat a question as often as necessary in order to help the young person give the proper responses.

An added advantage is that the learning program can be suited to the needs of each student. Frequently many different skills must be taught to such individuals, or their frustration will continue or increase. With teaching machines, each student can have his own individualized program and can work at his own speed.

Gadgets fascinate Americans of all ages. The teaching machine has enough appeal as a gadget to capture the interest of the most indifferent student, at least in the beginning. He is much more interested in learning to spell ten words with the machine than he would be if the teacher were to help him learn to spell the same ten words. Punctuation and capitalization hold more glamor on a machine than in a textbook. Capturing the interest of these slow learners is of primary importance. Most of them have experienced failure (and humiliation because of it) over and over again. Many have given up hope of learning. New hope and desire for academic learning must be generated in them. The teaching machine may be the answer for many young people.

Other educational machines are also being used to good effect with these slow learners. An overhead projector will illustrate, for example, the proper way to put a heading on an English paper, or a chart depicting diacritical marks while the students are working with dictionaries. Films and slides of all kinds, geared to the inter-

---

[4] *English Language Arts—The Fifth One:* The Star Series, Grades 10 and 11 (Austin, Texas: Austin Independent School District, 1961).

ests and understanding of the class, can make the written word come to life, serve as background information for reports, and make the abstract and general concrete and specific enough to be grasped.[5]

Reading. Reading is so often both cause and effect in retardation that some schools have turned their classes for slow achievers into remedial reading classes. Excellent materials with high interest and low vocabulary levels are available, often with helpful suggestions addressed to the learner or to the teacher. These may be comprehension exercises or special skill-building activities such as following a sequence of a story or skimming written material for specific facts.

Reading clinicians say that, in order to predict with some degree of accuracy whether a young person will profit from a concentrated program of reading skills, the teacher or counselor must know something about his ability to learn academic material. If he demonstrates by performance on a standardized intelligence test that he has an IQ of 80, this indicates that he probably is not capable of reading up to grade level. Perhaps he is already working at capacity. Intensive drill on skills will do very little good in that case. He does need further teaching and guidance in reading skills but these must be scaled to his ability to understand.

The person who ranks high on the intelligence test in nonverbal situations but drops way down in the verbal parts probably needs more intensive teaching in all language areas. If he is a very retarded reader and is highly motivated to overcome this, perhaps a crash program might be in order for him.

Unfortunately, not all remedial material is soundly conceived and executed. People with "panaceas" can sound very convincing to the uninformed. Some of the phonics materials have been particularly poorly conceived and poorly executed. These are seldom published by reputable companies but are sold in connection with three or more lectures by the author propagandizing his material. The cost is usually as high as that of good-quality, soundly based material.

Teaching machines of various kinds are also programmed for reading. Some of these such as the projectors which will show movies, filmstrips, and slides; or the machines, which use filmstrips

---

[5] For a more detailed discussion of this topic, see Robert E. De Kieffer, *Audio-visual Instruction* (New York: The Center for Applied Research in Education, 1965).

at controlled rates, can be used with the whole class or small groups. Other machines which pace the reading of printed materials are built for use by individual students. These machines are all designed primarily to increase reading rate. Some reading authorities call them *pushers*. Comprehension and vocabulary development, as well as many other skills, are taught through special materials (usually in workbook form).

Unfortunately, there are no simple formulas, no panaceas for teachers working with the slow achievers. It is hard work and always will be. Many of the newer teaching materials and gadgets alleviate the drudgery to an extent. Very good sequential programs are available. They have been worked out in detail by people who have a background of training and experience in teaching reading. The remedial materials usually have high interest appeal with low vocabulary level. The objective of these teaching aids is to capture the interest of the young person so he will be willing to read, and to teach him, in a palatable fashion, the skills he needs.

The Academically Talented

Since World War II, educators have become increasingly aware of the needs of the academically talented young people in our country. Sputnik I appeared to underline the importance of educating these young people to their fullest capacities. Now there is scarcely a high school where honors courses, ability grouping, or electives geared only to the most able are now proudly displayed in the curriculum.

Classes in which only the most able are admitted are sought after by most teachers. The assumption is that these young people will be eager to learn and are capable of unlimited understanding. Teachers and administrators tend to overlook the fact that even the brightest individual must be motivated to learn. True, there is a good chance that it will be easier to motivate the more able students, but these young people are also more skeptical of "gimmicks" and suspicious of "phonies." Many of them have the same emotional and psychological problems which may block or warp the learning of other adolescents.

Two general points of view have been taken toward the brighter student. One point of view maintains that these young people would learn anyway (in spite of the teacher if need be), that all that is really necessary is to turn them loose to explore. This is true in many cases, but many things are learned better when adequate guidance is provided. A verbally gifted adolescent may be able to write excellent reports or essays, but his writing could probably be improved by working with someone skilled in teaching composition. Teachers may not be essential for these academically talented youths, but competent teachers will furnish guidance to enhance and deepen the learning.

The other point of view asserts that the high school curriculum is geared to the able students. In the early part of the twentieth century, when high school curriculums were being fashioned, approximately 75 per cent of the students attending secondary school planned to go on to college. Consequently, the curriculum was planned to prepare them for college. Although many changes have since been made in the English curriculum, remnants of the old system are still to be found in current English textbooks. The material in the early textbooks was academically difficult (see Chapter I), and it was often required reading. As more and more students went on to high school, the textbooks and curricular requirements were changed somewhat. More modern writers are included, as well as more selections of direct appeal to young people. Some critics have charged that such selections do not hold enough challenge for the able student, that he should be exposed to more mature writing comparable to that generally found in college freshman and sophomore texts. This may be true, but the critics do not take into account that a college freshman is more mature than the high school senior. Adults often forget that the experiences of the later adolescent years can have profound effects on the way the adolescent views the world and himself.

As can be seen, there are arguments for both sides. Yet the fact remains that cultural forces have generated greater attention to the gifted student. Several patterns of organization have evolved. Probably the most common is homogeneous grouping. These classes are usually assigned either to well-established teachers or to the entire staff in rotation, almost never to the inexperienced or less able teachers. Some schools have outlined extra assignments over and above the regular course of study for these top-level classes. Special materials are ordered, often in paperback, and emphasis is placed on preparation for college. In the study of English for those able students, more grammar is often included than is expected of other classes, and special emphasis is given to expository writing. Other schools have simply left the teachers of these top classes free to do what they like. This, obviously, could be very good or very bad for the superior students, depending upon the teacher.

A second pattern is to establish a different English curriculum for the superior student. The "major works" classes in one school system admit only the most able students and those who are willing to work hard. This requirement tends to eliminate the academically lazy or those who are not highly motivated scholastically. A list of books, most of them in paperback editions, has been drawn up by a teacher committee for each grade level from nine through twelve. Books on this list are those which the teachers feel are worthwhile contributions to literature, will be comprehensible in terms of the adolescent experience, yet will stretch the individuals intellectually and emotionally. A half-dozen or more books serve as the basis for the year's work in English. Speaking and writing experiences are built around, and as a consequence of, the reading. Students act as literary critics, attempting to ascertain the author's purpose by analyzing his style and technique as well as his symbolism. The "major works" classes have proved very popular both among students and among parents.

The third method of organization for top-level English students is through special electives. A number of large high schools have long employed the practice of allowing sophomore students with a "B" average or better in English to enroll in special classes provided for able junior and senior students. Subjects such as drama, creative writing, world literature, and journalism are offered.

Many young people have special talents in these areas and develop rapidly when given an opportunity to pursue these special abilities. Other young people enjoy the opportunity of exploring relatively unknown fields. Their whole outlook is sometimes changed because of a deepened awareness of certain aspects of communication. For example, a student may be infinitely more appreciative of a well-written short story if he has himself attempted to write a short story and had his efforts carefully criticized by the teacher as well as by his fellow students. He may be more aware of what constitutes a fine dramatic performance on stage, television, or in the movies if he has had an opportunity to study a part in several plays and attempted to interpret the parts himself. These and similar kinds of experiences are generally challenging and broadening for students.

Some critics of the elective plan for able students say that these kinds of learnings should be available to all interested students regardless of their grade average or general ability. Many young people of average intelligence and with a modicum of interest in English show genuine talent in planning and producing stage sets; others show real promise as sports reporters or feature writers. Many believe that these young people with real talent should be given an opportunity to develop it regardless of such factors as general intelligence or scores on achievement tests.

The Average Achievers

The common, everyday variety of student is the one who has come in for the least consideration in recent years. In most schools the majority of students must be classified as average academically. Their achievement is satisfactory, yet not outstanding. When the school attempts to educate all kinds of young people, this is to be expected. Experience has shown that an alert and concerned teacher can do much to stimulate a slow learner, and that the academically gifted are capable of almost unlimited learning geared to their interests and talents. Less is known about the average student. Generally he is simply classified as mediocre: no one expects him to excel in anything, and he generally accepts this evaluation of his abilities.

We are just now coming to realize that many so-called average students are in reality underachievers. Somewhere along the way they have been labeled as "average" and have lost any real motivation for effort in learning. Nearly every adult has an acquaintance who excelled academically in college and who is very successful in his vocational field although in high school he showed no promise and nearly flunked English and everything else. When such persons are asked why they did not apply themselves earlier, their answers indicate that they fall into one of two categories: the "late bloomers," and those who had no academic motivation. The immature boy or girl may be slow to grasp concepts based on more mature experiences. He may not understand because he has not grown up as much as his classmates have, but given time and ample opportunities for experience, he may develop into a very productive learner later.

Every teacher dreams of inspiring the talented or being the interpreter of learning to the backward, but no one is particularly eager to teach the average adolescent. In spite of this lack of enthusiasm, the average group of learners in English represents the greatest educational problem. Will or does the general curriculum in English meet their language needs? What activities and learnings will bring real zest into the classroom situation? These are questions for which there are yet no adequate answers. If grouping is used, then it would seem that each level should have special attention, that each should have language activities and materials suited to its particular needs. Until we strengthen our teaching with more adequate over-all planning for students at all levels of academic ability, ability grouping will have grave weaknesses.

Special Problems of Teaching English

Because the learning and use of a language is so inextricably bound up with personality and emotional development, problems arise in the teaching of English which do not exist—or are not as severe—in other areas. Three such problems are: (1) teaching the non-English-speaking student; (2) dealing with emotionally disturbed young people; and (3) working effectively with remedial cases.

English as a second language. In several parts of the United States many children come to school neither speaking nor understanding English. If—as in southern Texas, New Mexico, or California—the non-English-speaking population is concentrated, there appears to be little need to learn English except that the school demands it. Frequently, too, these people are migrant laborers— picking cotton, thinning sugar beets, gathering fruits and vegetables. They move north or west with the crops in the spring and south and southeast again in the late fall. Many of the children are not in the school more than a few months each winter; the rest of the time they are on the road or laboring in the fields, hearing English only when they go to town for merchandise or when the overseer comes around.

Another problem lies in the fact that most non-English-speaking children are culturally disadvantaged through lack of verbalization in any language. Because conceptualization is based to such a large extent on language, words must be present in large measure for understanding the world around us. This is not the case in many of these migrant families. True, the members communicate with one another, but on a limited range of subjects and with limited vocabularies. The language they speak is not Spanish or Japanese, for example—but a sort of pidgin Spanish or Japanese with some elements of English, but based upon only a meager vocabulary.

It is not uncommon for the migrant child to enter the seventh grade at age fifteen and be unable to tell where he has been during the past eight months or much of what he did or saw. Travel has not broadened his knowledge, principally because no one in the group had the words to point things out. Simple, everyday words concerning the most rudimentary experiences are not understood until the individual has a chance to experience these things together with much verbalization. For example, the word *clean* does not hold the same meaning for a child whose parents have verbalized over and over again the need for washing one's hands before meals or after touching something dirty as it does for a child for whom personal hygiene consists of only an occasional washing of hands with inadequate soap and water and who hears little said about the process. Even children from homes where comparatively little attention is paid to cleanliness will absorb the ideas which generally prevail through hearing others talk about being clean, provided they have contact with other people who demonstrate meaning through their actions as well as through their words.

Numerous plans have been tried in teaching the non-English-speaking student, but none of them has proved too successful as yet. One solution is to give children entering elementary school a year of concrete language training in which they have the opportunity to explore many things in the world that they never came in contact with before. Things such as tricycles, farm animals, common household utensils, and tableware are used in play and in vocabulary drill. The children dramatize the Mother Goose rhymes and take the parts of characters in American folk tales such as the Three Little Pigs, Little Red Riding Hood, or the Three Bears.

When they enter first grade, the non-English-speaking children are placed in rooms with English-speaking children. After this intensive training in verbalized experience, these children usually have enough command of English to be able to communicate with their classmates and their teacher in that language. If they are allowed by their parents to remain in school for the full school year, these children generally do remarkably well. They learn to read and write in English to a limited degree and their English vocabularies expand rapidly.

Even though this program does make it possible for non-English-speaking children to enter first-grade classes with at least some idea of what is expected of them, they are often so far behind that only the brightest can keep up with the others. Competency in reading and in vocabulary development may be inadequate for the average child to progress from one grade to the next. He becomes discouraged and often stops trying to learn English. By the time these children reach secondary school, usually one of two things has happened: some of them have improved their verbal skills to a point at which they can compete and participate successfully with their classmates in academic learning; the others have become so discouraged with their academic progress that they feel the whole endeavor is futile. These hopeless ones are often absent from school. If they become too frustrated they will become behavior problems in school or withdraw into their own private worlds where English makes no difference. Both groups—the troublemakers and the silent ones—will drop out of school as soon as they legally can. The sad part is that these children leave school knowing neither English nor any other language well enough to be really literate, and they will probably perpetuate the verbal problem through their children.

Some schools set up special English classes in the seventh, eighth, and ninth grades for students who have little facility in English. Sometimes these classes run for two or three periods a day. In such cases, the teacher attempts to teach some health, social studies, or science concepts through the work in English. Time is spent in discussing where the children have been, what they have done, and how they feel about such things. Field trips to a newspaper plant or to a television studio are valuable experiences. Writing is taught from the functional point of view, in an attempt to help these young people face the problems of writing letters, filling out application blanks, or making grocery lists.

Classes which attempt to build language skills rapidly must be kept small. Teaching of this kind cannot be done in large groups. Individual and small-group teaching is the principal method. A teacher who works with non-English-speaking children must understand their backgrounds, must realize how they feel and why, and must be convinced that these seemingly backward students can learn if given a real chance. Many schools require the teachers of English for non-English-speaking students to be able to speak their native language. This helps to build a common bond between the young people and the teacher, and fosters mutual respect for both languages.

The criticism hurled against the grouping together all of the non-English-speaking children is that this is a form of segregation, and the students have no model for their English but the teacher. There is little time for fraternizing with English-speaking students, so that the separation may set up barriers to communication between the two groups. When this happens, much of the value is lost because resistance to learning English begins to develop.

Much research needs to be done on the problem of teaching English to non-English-speaking students. This is an area in which teachers of modern languages and English must cooperate in giving guidance to the public schools. Local experimentation is fine, but without the research there is little assurance that new arrangements will be any better than the old.

Emotionally disturbed children and language. Frequently, when the verbal score on standardized tests is markedly lower than nonverbal scores, the teacher or counselor surmises that the child has had or is having some emotional problem. Research has shown that an emotionally disturbed child will often have more difficulty than a normal child in learning to read. It is also true that many children who do not learn to read easily or effectively develop emotional problems.

Because language may be both the cause and the effect of emotional maladjustment, it must be handled with knowledge of possible consequences. To insist that an unusually shy individual give a lengthy report before the class may upset him so much that he develops a complete (though temporary) blockage of memory or even a stammer. On the other hand, this young person needs language in order to overcome his extreme shyness. Therefore he must be encouraged to report briefly to small groups, to read short announcements to the class, or to participate vocally in any way in situations where he feels a minimum of threat. Sometimes a combined reading and oral-participation program can be devised for the shy students. Books which deal with similar personal problems, such as Cavanna's *Going on Sixteen* or Cronin's *Shannon's Way*, may serve as the basis for a conference with the teacher or as a device for sharing ideas about books with a small group of classmates. The shy student not only has a book to talk about, but he also can discuss the problem of the heroine or hero with considerable insight yet with objectivity as well.

Gray and Rogers, in their research on maturity in reading, discovered that the person who is classified as mature also communicates more with other people in all ways than the less mature reader.[6] This finding indicates that effective communication is essential in helping young people to mature in all respects. The old concept that the bright, shy boy was probably a genius is not borne out in reality. We now know that the bright boy who communicates well is likely to be much more successful. It takes facility in communication, both oral and written, to solve a complex problem effectively. The right questions must be asked if the right answers are to be found. Clear explanations must be sought to ascertain whether what is discovered is reasonable. Above all, the student must be able to report in understandable terms to his colleagues—and even to the world—what he has learned. This takes expert language facility.

The English curriculum should never be saddled with the attempt to solve all the emotional problems of students. But curriculum-makers should keep in mind that adolescence is a period of change, turmoil, and adjustment, and if young people are to be served adequately, their personal problems through and with their language must be dealt with.

Remedial language problems. The problems of children who develop inadequacies in some phase of language vary tremendously. A child with low intellectual ability will never be as effective a reader or speaker as those who have average or superior ability. Such a child, then, is not a proper subject for remedial teaching. Only those persons judged to be capable of performing at a significantly higher verbal level than their present level can be classified as remedial.

---

[6] William S. Gray and Bernice Rogers, *Maturity in Reading: Its Nature and Appraisal* (Chicago: The University of Chicago Press, 1956).

Research evidence indicates that the performance of many of these children can be improved through remedial teaching.

A good remedial program has a number of characteristics. First, only qualified people who have had special training in teaching remedial speaking, listening, reading, and writing, and who work easily with boys and girls should be employed to teach remedial classes. In a large system which can support it, a special language clinic with trained clinicians may also be needed.

Second, the problems of the person needing remedial help should be very carefully diagnosed. This diagnosis must contain not only an analysis of his verbal problems; it should also point up any physical, social, or emotional difficulties which may be evident. Often, when some physical difficulty is overcome, the remedial work becomes twice as effective. When a hearing loss is discovered and a hearing aid is used by the student, for example, the reading or speech problem will—with remedial help—disappear rapidly.

Other problems, such as loss of a parent through death or divorce, are not so easily remedied. If the teacher is aware of the child's problem, however, he may be more effective in his efforts to solve it.

Problems of verbal learning may be caused by many factors. Often there is no single cause but a complex of causes which should be understood before teaching can be effective. Although some retardation in reading and writing may be the result of poor teaching, this is seldom the sole factor. Treating the verbal disabilities may produce good results, but the results will be better if all factors of cause are known and understood.

Third, teaching practices that are both pedagogically and psychologically sound should be employed. This rules out fads and gimmicks which self-styled experts sometimes try to sell to a school system. Crash programs in rapid reading or phonics may do more harm than good. Many children and young people need much work on comprehension skills, such as understanding the organization of an essay or recognizing figurative language, before they can increase their reading speed.

Much study has been done on remedial teaching. Excellent materials have been produced to assist in the process. Hundreds of books have been written on the subject. Many colleges of education in large universities have reading, speech, and hearing clinics which serve as training centers for clinicians and provide expert help for children and young people. Some public schools have teams of trained people to deal with these special problems for several schools or for the whole system.

Non-English-speaking children, emotionally disturbed learners, and students in need of remedial work are pressing problems in many English classrooms, but there are other problems as well. We know much about teaching reading and we know some things about working with emotionally blocked or disturbed children, but we know very little about teaching the culturally disadvantaged students for whom English is not a native tongue, or about improving the writing skills of those who cannot express themselves adequately on paper. The composition problem is still under study and perhaps we may have some real answers to these problems relatively soon. A start has been made on research on teaching the culturally disadvantaged, but little study has been undertaken on the non-English-speaking adolescent. There is still much to be done in the whole area of meeting individual language problems.

CHAPTER IV

English in Grades 7, 8, and 9

Up until the early 1900's, the almost universal pattern of public education in America was an eight-grade elementary school and a four-year secondary school. At the turn of the century many educators were agitating for a stronger secondary school to prepare students for college more adequately. President Eliot of Harvard, along with many others, helped to start the movement of reorganization. One of the recommendations to come out of several study groups formed during this period was the six-year secondary school. This led in turn to the establishment of the junior high school.

Beginnings and Growth of the Junior High School

The school year 1909–10 is usually said to mark the beginning of the junior high school movement. In that year two school systems—Columbus, Ohio, and Berkeley, California—introduced the 6–3–3 plan. Many school systems were so impressed with the results of the Columbus and Berkeley experiments that educators felt that the junior high school might be the answer to the problem of reorganization. After World War I secondary school enrollments increased rapidly, doubling and redoubling in a very short time. The greatest gain was in the number of children staying on through the ninth grade. Junior high school buildings were especially designed for the needs of the new program.

In spite of the impression of universality of junior high schools in America, there are many, many variations of the system. Some schools retain the 8–4 system; some have a 6–6 system which lengthens the secondary school program but ignores the separation between the junior and senior high school levels. Conant, in his report on the junior high school, says:

> I have found great diversity with respect to the place of Grades 7 and 8 in the organization of school systems. . . . Indeed, there appears no end to the variety of organizational schemes in which I

56

have found Grades 7 and 8, a situation which an observer fifty years ago would not have found.[1]

Although there is no consistent junior high school pattern in the United States, the rationale from which the movement gained impetus is still far-reaching in the stated and implied purposes of education in Grades 7, 8, and 9.

A large group of educators felt that the new junior high school could be geared more directly to the needs of young adolescents. If this were done, they felt, learning would be more effective and it might also reduce the number of children from dropping out between Grades 7, 8, and 9. In 1916 Frank Bunker reported:

> Of every one hundred children annually entering the first grade of our schools, practically all reach the end of the fifth grade. Between this point and the first year of high school, from 60 to 67 per cent of those reaching fifth grade will be lost. . . .[2]

In 1956, 89 per cent of the children aged twelve to fifteen were enrolled in school. Numerous factors account for this phenomenal rise of universal secondary education, but the fact remains that it occurred after the junior high school movement became an integral part of the American school system and focused increased attention to the special needs of young adolescents.

The advocates of the junior high school feel that the subject content of the junior high school should be adapted to the interests, aptitudes, and developmental stages of the students. The present-day English curriculum in most schools reflects this aim to a considerable degree. Literature books and readers (see Chapter II) contain many selections which will appeal directly to boys and girls of this developmental level. Composition assignments are generally based on their reactions to the stories read or on their own daily activities.

A second principle evident in the movement was that the junior high school should provide a smooth transition between elementary school and high school. The aim was to strike a balance between the child-centered approach of the first six grades and the subject-matter

---

[1] James Bryant Conant, *A Memorandum to School Boards: Recommendations for Education in the Junior High School Years* (Princeton, N.J.: Educational Testing Service, 1960), p. 10.

[2] Frank F. Bunker, *Reorganization of the Public School System*, U.S. Office of Education Bulletin No. 8 (Washington, D.C.: USGPO, 1916), p. 101. Cited in William T. Gruhn and Harl R. Douglass, *The Modern Junior High School* (New York: The Ronald Press Company, 1956), p. 16.

approach of the upper levels. Teachers were employed who were better grounded in a given subject area than the usual elementary school teacher. On the other hand, more emphasis was placed on knowing and understanding the young adolescent and gearing the subject matter to his level and interests than was true of the typical high school. Departmentalization became the prevalent organizational structure.

The third principle or premise, closely allied to the second, is that the junior high school should provide appropriate activities for young adolescents. As adolescence sets in, the needs of the individual change. He demands participation in active sports, yet he must be protected against physical harm. Adolescent girls become sex conscious, and need the wholesome social outlet of coed group parties. Both sexes need opportunity to explore widely their many fields of interest through hobbies, clubs, class activities, and reading. These young adolescents are a group apart, with special needs and interests which the school should help meet.

Special Needs of Young Adolescents Which Concern Language Development

Young adolescents may be likened to quicksilver: the least little change can disturb their equilibrium. The physical changes rampant during this period set off a chain reaction in emotional, social, and intellectual areas. Because language is an integral part of the personality and because mastery over language is important for the well-being and growth of the individual, English teachers have a special—and, some feel, an arduous—task. It is a challenging task and a rewarding one when the teacher understands both the nature of language and that of the young adolescent.

The expanding world and language. Because of the new world of adult activities which opens to him with his growing physical maturity, the young adolescent becomes aware of many things around him he had never noticed before. Different, more responsible behavior is expected of him, and he is sometimes at a loss to know how he should behave. New relationships between himself and his parents, his brothers and sisters, his peers, and adults in general are all bewildering.

Language is essential in the process of gaining new perspectives.

Vocabulary expansion—in terms of both new or expanded meanings for old words and new terms to describe and understand the new experiences—is important to the young adolescent. This is a period of experimentation with language, as can be seen in the slang and special vocabularies each new generation invents for itself. Young adolescents derive much pleasure from the sound of words, from unusual words or onomatopoetic words, from a well-turned phrase, from a play on words.

Junior high school boys and girls follow special interests or fads avidly and single-mindedly. Many young girls want to read all there is to read about horses, young love, or careers. Many boys devour sports stories, sea stories, or westerns. Early adolescence may well be called the age of reading. It is not uncommon to find in this age group boys and girls who read from fifty to one hundred fifty books a year. Reading is their method of exploring the world around them, of finding out how it feels to win or lose, of discovering how other adolescents or young adults solve their problems. For some, reading becomes a substitute for direct experience: it is less painful to live in a world of fictional characters than it is to live among other teen-agers and adults who do not treat them with understanding.

During the past thirty to forty years, many books and stories written especially for young adolescents have been published. Books for young people are relative newcomers to the field of literature, developing only since World War I. It is difficult for a teacher or librarian to keep up with the flood of books currently being turned out.

What of the quality of this material? Although only a relatively small number of these thousands of books can be considered really fine literature, the general caliber of works in this field seems to be constantly improving. Most of the books are far superior to the *Hardy Boys* or *Nancy Drew* of a generation or two ago, or even to Harold Bell Wright or Gene Stratton Porter's overly sentimental novels. Books such as Maureen Daly's *Seventeenth Summer,* Mary Stolz's *To Tell Your Love* or *Pray Love, Remember,* Esther Forbes' *Johnny Tremain,* Armstrong Sperry's *Call It Courage,* or John Tunis' *All-American* are all well written, yet deal with the kinds of problems or interests which young adolescents have and understand. By reading books such as these, boys and girls gain real insights into the satisfactions and enjoyment literature can bring. This appreciation brings them to the point of accepting and understanding the more mature literature which they will meet in senior high school.

The junior high years are truly years of exploration and experimentation. The English teacher will do well to be prepared to guide this exploration through books that open new vistas for young adolescents.

The need for better control over environment. Frustration is a fairly normal state for many young adolescents. They often lack full control over their growing bodies. They may have the size and strength for many physical activities, but they lack the skill and coordination to carry through such activities. They want the approbation of their peers, yet they frequently act in a belligerent and hostile way toward their friends.

Most of these young people do not yet possess the verbal skills to bridge the gap between themselves and others. One of the greatest contributions English teachers can make to these frustrated and bewildered children is to provide direct, concrete guidance in developing the skills to communicate effectively. They must learn to use language to persuade, to explain, to express feelings, to understand what the other person is saying. This is the essence of English for Grades 7, 8, and 9.

The need for every child to develop into an effective and integrated adult. As was pointed out in Chapter I, each individual must be valued for his own worth in a democratic society. Each must be given the opportunity of developing his own special potentials and talents. Language and the control of language are necessary for the integration and full development of a personality. If one frequently feels at cross purposes with himself and others because he cannot adequately express his feelings, he will be at an impasse until he accidentally discovers for himself—or until someone with understanding and skill shows him—better methods and different patterns of language communication than those he currently possesses.

Acquisition of knowledge is greatly affected by the way the personality is developed. A happy, outgoing individual who has faith in himself and in others learns more readily than one who is unhappy, frustrated, and at odds with himself and the world.

The need for a variety of activities. Physical change in young adolescents frequently results either in an unusual amount of activity or in sluggishness and apparent apathy. Both conditions can be disturbing to the adult, but both will pass eventually. Such behavior is difficult to cope with while it lasts. One of the most constructive ways of dealing with it in the English classroom is through a variety of methods and activities which are centered on the interests and concerns of the students. A classroom in which drill without understanding or reading without much comprehension is found will be rife with rebellion brought on by frustration and boredom. In contrast, a classroom in which young people are engaged in using language to help plan their classwork for the next week, or in which an exciting story is being dramatized by the group who read it while the rest listen for agreed-upon points, will be a relaxed, pleasant place where communication is easy.

One of the advantages of teaching English is the vast amount and endless variety of materials and methods which are applicable to the task. The exposure of young minds and spirits to a variety of experiences increases their backgrounds and perceptions. It also affords opportunity for students with different talents, abilities, and interests to express themselves. Variety is not only the "spice of life," it is also the essence of English learning.

The need for aesthetic experience. Every culture has its own standards of beauty. All men appear to have a need to experience something that—through its form, color, or pattern—gives the spirit a lift. This aesthetic experience is important to the young adolescent's development. He needs to take pride in helping to produce a lovely object or pleasant sounds. Fine prose as well as good poetry can convey an aesthetic feeling, either in the reading or in the writing of it. To help young people discover this experience is obviously one of the tasks of the English teacher. Too frequently children do not develop an aesthetic appreciation until they are given some guidance and help.

There is much in our literary heritage that can spark the feeling of true enjoyment in young adolescents—Vachel Lindsay's "The Congo," Esther Forbes' *Johnny Tremain,* Mark Twain's *Tom Sawyer* or *Huckleberry Finn,* Frost's "Stopping by Woods." These and many other selections can produce many wonderful feelings of beauty and well-being.

The young adolescent is often a producer of good-quality prose or poetry, if he is given the necessary encouragement to try. Even when he knows the product is not perfect, he will have real pride in what he produces if the teacher is sympathetic and understanding. He will also gain a new appreciation of what it takes to write well and he will be more attentive to details and devices established authors use to produce certain effects.

Aesthetic experiences may serve as an important outlet for the tension and strain which often build up in young people. They can do much to release tensions and relax tight nerves while they stimulate or even exhilarate.

Curricular Organization of Junior High School English

All types of curricular structure (see Chapter II) can be found in junior high school English programs. It is not uncommon for two daily class periods to be devoted to the language arts at the seventh- and eighth-grade levels. For example, one period might be devoted to written and oral language skills (including spelling, grammar, and usage), while the other might be used for increasing efficiency in reading skills. (Of course, the skills may be taught independently of one another in one-period arrangements also.)

Scope-and-sequence skills approach. The content to be taught in this subject-centered organization is determined primarily either by the textbooks selected for spelling, reading, and so forth, or by a scope-and-sequence chart drawn up by the state department of public instruction (as in Maryland[3]) or by a committee of supervisors and English teachers (as in San Francisco[4] or Denver[5]). *Flexibility* is the key word used in the discussion of these charts. A Maryland bulletin says, "Concepts in the language arts should be developed gradually and consistently. . . . Growth in language requires a sequential development of skills from Grades 1 through

---

[3] *Planning for Effective Learning: Language Arts* (Annapolis, Md.: State Department of Education for the Superintendent's Committee on Curriculum Supervision, 1956).

[4] *Framework for Secondary School English,* Progress Report of Committee on Curriculum Problems in Secondary English (San Francisco: San Francisco Unified School District, 1954).

[5] *A Program in English: A Guide for Teaching the Language Arts: Kindergarten Through Grade 12* (Denver: The Department of Instruction, 1953).

12."[6] In a study of English as taught in American high schools, Arno Jewett states:

> Almost all courses of study included in the present survey provide programs which have a definite sequential pattern, especially in grammar and usage, spelling, punctuation, and reading. More recent courses of study offer a flexible scope-and-sequence pattern in all the language arts. These courses repeatedly emphasize that the program must be adapted to the individual's present levels of achievement, maturity, ability, and his purposes and needs.[7]

One major advantage of this organization is the assurance that all the skills, in accordance with developmental-growth patterns, have been covered. This avoids the danger of overlooking an important skill because it did not fit easily into the fused or core pattern.

The principal weakness of the separate-skills approach is that these skills, when learned in isolation, are difficult for children to apply in other situations and motivation is more difficult. This is the reason so many schools are following the unit approach without disregarding the necessity for sequential development of skills.

Fused programs of English. Because transfer of learning does not seem to occur automatically, psychologists and curriculummakers have urged that content to be learned be put into its natural or proper setting. For example, punctuation rules should be applied to composition work, and learning to participate effectively in a group discussion should be related to a problem or situation of real concern and importance to the learner. The student is likely to be much more careful of his punctuation if he knows that what he writes will be printed or at least be read by others besides the teacher.

Another curriculum term for a fused program is *broad fields.* Both terms imply that all the language arts are interrelated and should be taught in such a way that this interrelatedness is apparent and mutually reinforcing.

The broad-fields program of language arts in Grades 7, 8, and 9 relates reading skills to literature and essay-type material, literature to composition (through writing about what has been read), compo-

---

6 *Planning for Effective Learning: Language Arts, op. cit.,* p. 1.
7 Arno Jewett, *English Language Arts in American High Schools,* U.S. Office of Education Bulletin No. 13 (Washington, D.C.: USGPO, 1958), p. 50.

sition to speaking (either before or after the writing), and speaking to listening (through evaluation of what the speaker has said and how). No aspect of the language is taught as a separate and discrete knowledge or skill. Emphasis is placed upon the interdependence of the various elements—how spelling aids composition and how composition is dependent upon vocabulary and critical thinking.

The fused program may be organized around blocks of work such as composition (including punctuation, spelling, and usage), reading (including the basic skills, discussion of characters or points of view implied), and composition as a result of the reading. This is a subject-centered approach to the fused program.

The fused program may also be organized around units. Junior high school English units are generally centered around themes of interest and concern to young adolescents or their developmental needs. This organization often combines the child-centered approach of the elementary school and the subject-centered approach of the high school, blending them to suit the transitional period of early adolescence.

Core programs and English.   The term *core* in curricular parlance has a number of meanings. For purposes of this discussion, the definition used in the Indiana Curriculum Bulletin will apply:

> *Core:* An extended period of time is scheduled for an instructional program which is organized in terms of adolescent, personal-social, and societal needs; of integrated subject areas; or of experiences that may be considered as the nucleus or main portion of the child's school experience.[8]

In this type of organization, the subject content of English and that of the social studies are often combined, although any subject field which contributes to the study of the problem—music, art, science, or mathematics—is usually included. Language skills are applied to all the work on the unit, whether it be planning, reporting orally or in writing on a particular problem, discussing the pros and cons of a decision to be made, or inviting a citizen of the community to talk to the class. Time out for drill on particularly troublesome punctuation, spelling, or usage problems is generally provided when the teacher and students think it profitable.

---

[8] *The Junior High School,* State of Indiana Department of Public Instruction Bulletin No. 246 (1961), p. 24.

Typical topics for core classes in the junior high school are "Orientation to the Junior High School," "Animals and How They Help Us," "Sports and Recreation in America," "How People Earn a Living and Spend Their Money," "People Who Helped Build America," "Life and People of Other Countries," "Understanding One's Family," "It's the Way You Do Things That Counts: Manners, Etiquette, and Behavior," and "Pioneers, Then and Now."

At first glance, very little English as such appears to be included in these core-unit topics. How can one be sure that composition skills, for example, will be covered under these topics? Does English become a mere handmaiden in this kind of arrangement? These questions reveal real concerns about the core plan. Unless the teacher is well grounded in the language skills and their development in young adolescents, there is a danger that these skills will not be as well learned as they need to be. There is also the danger that the opportunity for aesthetic experiences which should be furnished in the English classroom may be overlooked.

The core unit does provide ample opportunity for meaningful, functional encounters of language. Motivation for learning the skills necessary to perform and to learn more effectively is increased when their real purpose is made evident. The integration of the various skills in problem-solving gives these young people a workable method for learning about other things of vital concern to them. Problems in real life are not divided into those of mathematics, science, social studies, or English. All these subject disciplines are necessary for the solution of most real-life problems.

The type of core class described here can be found in relatively few junior high schools in America today. Although the concept has been advocated for about thirty years, not much has been done in most institutions of higher learning to prepare teachers to handle core classes. The profession as well as the public does not readily understand a totally new concept of curricular organization. They are apt to be hesitant to institute anything new or different which they themselves have not had an opportunity to experience.

Quite a number of junior high schools in all parts of the country attempt some kind of correlation of subject matter, however. The combination of social studies and English is the most common, although that of science and mathematics can be found also. Under this arrangement, a teacher works with a class for two or more (preferably consecutive) periods. He is responsible for teaching the subject content of both courses. Sometimes each is taught independently, each subject being studied for a set period each day. Other schools attempt some integration of the two fields, at least in the skill aspects. Some teachers blend the two subjects, keeping a flexible schedule which will provide for the group's needs in both fields. In this arrangement, the units are generally drawn from the social studies material. For example, in Austin, Texas, where this double assignment is prevalent for seventh-grade classes in social studies and language arts, the main theme of study is Texas in all its phases—historical, geographical, governmental—with additional units on "Orientation to the Junior High School" and "Life in Latin America." The amount of integration is left up to the teacher, although maximum relation of the subject fields is recommended.

The weaknesses of the correlation plan are easily seen. It is difficult to find teachers who are equally well prepared in English and in the social studies. The social studies curriculum generally predominates in the material used for study. The aesthetic aspects of the field are likely to be disregarded altogether.

The strengths of the plan are also evident. The child leaving the self-contained classroom of the elementary school adjusts more readily to the junior high school and departmentalization if he has one teacher who knows him well enough to give him the help he often needs. Besides, there is one less personality to adjust to in the new and more complex world of the junior high school. The teacher can give more assistance to students who need help in the basic skills, especially the skills of reading and composition. He can compare the students' performance in one area with that in another, and can reinforce his teaching in both situations. The learning time can be organized more flexibly to meet individual differences than in a one-hour period each day.

Unit Teaching in the Junior High School

The term *unit* has gained such popularity among English teachers that they are apt to use it indiscriminately to describe skill-building in reading, a series of spelling lessons, or a study of the pronoun in all its ramifications. These are scarcely topics or content for units. Of course, these skills and knowledges will be included in unit teaching, but the topic of the unit must have the following character-istics: (1) It should be related to some interest, concern, or develop-mental need of the student, with real significance for the learner and for his society. (2) It should be broad enough in scope to provide for a wide range of individual interests and needs typical among adolescents. (3) It should provide material for more than a couple of class periods of work. At least two weeks is usually spent on a topic, although the time may run into eight or even ten weeks for broad major themes. (4) It should furnish the kinds of learning ex-periences which require a wide variety of learning materials as well as language skills.

Jewett reports that the units found in numerous state and city language-arts guides are related "to a significant educational pur-pose, a basic need or human problem, a theme, a famous author and his works, a communications job, or a literary type of interest and value to students."[9]

Fairly typical titles of language-arts units are the following drawn from the Minnesota guide,[10] San Francisco, California, guide,[11] and the Katy, Texas, guide:[12]

Seventh Grade:
"Wonder Workers"
"Animal Parade"
"Becoming Acquainted with School"
"Changing Styles in Heroes and Heroines"
"Growing up in Other Lands"
"Wonders of Science and Invention"
"Long Ago and Far Away"
Eighth Grade:
"Mind Your Manners"
"What's on Tonight?"
"Hobbies, Sports and Sportsmanship"
"Adventuring in Books"
"Getting Along with Others"
"Who are Americans?"
"What Is Success?"

---

9 Jewett, *op. cit.,* p. 51.
10 *A Guide for Instruction in the Language Arts: Secondary School, Grades 7–12,* Curriculum Bulletin No. 18 (St. Paul: State of Minnesota Department of Education, 1956).
11 *Framework for Secondary School English, loc. cit.*
12 *A Resource Guide for English Language Arts: Secondary School, Grades 7 and 8; 9 and 10* (Katy, Texas: Katy Independent School District, 1959).

"At Work and at Play"
"Reading the Ads"
Ninth Grade:
"Families Are Like That"
"Planning for a Job"
"Living in an Air Age"
"Understanding Ourselves and Others"
"One World through Books"
"The One-Act Play"
"As Good as Your Word"
"Teen-Age Problems"
"Wanted: Good Friends"
"Magazines"

Just how are units organized? What kinds of learning activities are included? How do you evaluate what is learned? These and other similar questions can best be answered by examining a sample language-arts resource unit drawn up and used by teachers in the Katy, Texas, Independent School District. The resource unit was designed for the ninth grade:

Teen-age Problems

I. *Objectives*
    A. Knowledge, concepts, attitudes:
        To discover the most common problems of teen-agers and some possible methods of solution.
        To realize that many problems are not peculiar to a few individuals, but are common to many teen-agers.
        To gain a better understanding of ourselves, our peers, and our parents.
        To become aware of faulty types of thinking.
        To realize that overcoming faulty types of thinking is an important aid in solving problems.
    B. Skills:
        To become better able to recognize and solve individual problems.
        To read to gain information for solving problems.
        To relate reading experiences to real-life situations.
        To participate in small-group and class discussions.
        To use correctly the cases of pronouns.
II. *Suggested Activities*
    A. Initiatory:
        Begin by reading "The Apprentice" . . . in *Adventures in Reading*. Discuss the selection.

What was Peg's problem? Was it real? Do teen-agers today experience the same feelings? How does Rollie help her to understand her parents? Any satisfactory selection dealing with teen-age problems may be chosen as an approach to the unit.

Have groups of students set up lists of personal problems.

Let the groups exchange problems and offer solutions.

Keep a list of these problems for later reference.

Assign library books, fiction or nonfiction, to be read during the unit.

B. Developmental:

Read and discuss material in "Thinking It Out," *English in Action, Course 1.* . . . List the types of faulty thinking on the board as they are discussed.

Have each student write of an incident where he knows he has used some type of erroneous thinking.

Have the students read the selections for the unit and discuss each orally or in writing.

Have the students point out the faulty thinking on the part of characters. For instance, in "You've Got to Learn," what type of wrong thinking did Andy Gates use? How did he finally see his error? How did his mother and father feel about his search for the otter? Do you think his feelings and behavior in such a situation typical of a teen-ager? Can you personally understand Andy?

Select vocabulary from reading selections for the unit. Have students define them in context if possible.

Check into available guidance services offered by the school. Do students feel a need for such services? Do they know whom to go to for help on personal problems?

Stimulate a class discussion by formulating a set of questions on boy-girl problems. Sample questions:

1. Should there be a curfew for dates on school nights?
2. Should a girl ever call up a boy?
3. Often boys do not take the initiative at our school dances. Should girls ask the boys to dance?
4. Should a boy or girl break a date for the prom to go with someone else?

Set up some problem situations for sociodrama. Do not use more than three or four situations in one class period. Have students assume the roles of the people in the situation. Sample situations:

1. Mary has invited everyone in her circle of friends, except Sally, to a hamburger fry in her backyard. Sally does not know if she has been left out [through] an oversight or on purpose. All the girls have been chattering about the expected good time during physical education class. At the end of the class, Mary and Sally find themselves alone together in the shower room. What would these two say to each other and how would they act?

2. John and Jean have been going steady for six months, but before the prom John asked Ellen to be his date for the prom, the big event of the year. At the prom, Jean and John are seated next to each other while the iradtes are dancing with someone else. How do you suppose they acted, and what did they say?

Let the class members react to the situations as they are portrayed.

Discuss individual reading of novels in class often enough to keep up interest and to share reading experiences with one another. Questions for discussion: What problem or problems did the character in your book have? How did he solve them? Do you think the solution was satisfactory? Do problems such as the character in the book had ever occur in real life? Do you think problems could be solved in a similar way in real life?

Use "How to Solve Personal Problems" in *Be a Better Reader, Book III,* . . . as an activity.

From the error cards kept on students and from compositions, make a list of all pronoun errors. Then teach to correct these errors. Also stress terminology of grammar related to pronouns such as the following:

Personal pronouns
Compound personal pronouns
Case—nominative, objective, possessive
Indefinite pronouns
Agreement with antecedent
Usage

C. Culminating:

Divide the class into groups and return the teen-age-problem lists to them for possible solutions.

This should register any improvements made in their thinking and their solution of problems.

If the students still feel a need for finding solutions and understanding of problems they cannot solve, a parent-student panel to get varying points of view might be helpful. Points for discussion should come from previous student discussions in class.

Write a paper on the main character in your library book. Tell what his or her greatest problem was and how it was solved. Do you think the solution was satisfactory? Why, or why not?

Write a paper on one of the following, or a similar topic.

The Family Car and I

The Way I Keep My Room

How I Feel About My Room

The Way I Take Care of My Clothes

Why I Want a Job

What Time Should Teen-Agers Come Home?

How My Parents Could Help Me Be a Better Person

How My Teachers Could Help Me Be a Better Person

III. *Suggested Evaluation*

Have the students write an evaluation of the unit in terms of recognition and possible solution of their personal problems.

Give a test over the material read and studied stressing problems and their solutions. Sample question:

In the story, "You've Got to Learn," Andy Gates' actions were governed by a wrong type of thinking for quite some time. What was the wrong type of thinking he used? Explain why he used it. Also explain how his thinking changed.

Give a test on the correct use of pronouns stressing case and agreement with antecedent.

IV. *Suggested Materials*

A. Teacher:

Crawford, John E., and Luther E. Woodward. *Better Ways of Growing Up*. Muhlenberg.

Gardner, Gladys, *et al. Teen-Agers*. Scott, Foresman.

Landis, Paul H. *Adolescence and Youth*. McGraw.

Schacter, Helen. *How Personalities Grow*. McKnight.

Schacter, Helen, *et al. Into Your Teens*. Scott, Foresman.

Smith, Nila Banton. *Be a Better Reader, Book III*. Prentice.

Tressler, J. C. and Henry I. Christ. "Getting Along with People," in *English in Action, Course 2*. Heath, 1955. p. 3.

————. "Personality and Human Relations," in *English in Action, Course 4*. Heath, 1955. p. 20.

B. Text:

Adventures in Reading

Benet. "Portrait of a Boy," p. 270.

Callaghan. "Luke Baldwin's Vow," p. 170.

Canfield. "The Apprentice," p. 106.
Foote. "The Dancers," p. 486.
Murphy. "You've Got to Learn," p. 127.
Pooler. "Shago," p. 154.
West. "Trademark," p. 46.
English in Action, Course 1
"Thinking It Out," p. 192.
"Using Correct Pronouns," p. 328.
C. Supplementary:
Individual reading
Allen, Merritt P. *Spirit of the Eagle.* Longmans.
Archibald, Jo. *Rebel Halfback.* Macrae Smith.
Berry, Erick. *Green Door to the Sea.* Viking.
Bishop, Curtis. *Hero at Halfback.* Steck.
Brown, Christy. *My Left Foot.* Simon.
Cavanna, Betty. *Going on Sixteen.* Westminster.
Chute, B. J. *Blocking Back.* Macmillan.
Cormack, Maribelle. *Swamp Boy.* McKay.
Cory, Paul. *Shad Haul.* Morrow.
Cronin, A. J. *The Green Years.* Little.
Dickson, Marguerite. *Bramble Bush.*
———. *Only Child.*
———. *Roof Over Our Heads.*
Douglas, John Scott. *Secret of the Undersea Bell.* Dodd.
du Jardin, Rosamond. *Double Date.* Lippincott.
———. *Double Feature.* Lippincott.
Emery, Ann. *Going Steady.* Westminster.
———. *Mountain Laurel.* Westminster.
———. *Scarlet Royal.* Westminster.
———. *Senior Year.* Westminster.
Farley, Walter. *Blood Bay Colt.* Random.
———. *Son of Black Stallion.* Random.
Frank, Anne. *The Diary of a Young Girl.* Doubleday.
Gorsline, Douglas. *Farm Boys.* Viking.
Gray, Elizabeth. *Sandy.* Viking.
Howard, Elizabeth. *A Girl of the North Country.* Morrow.
Rendina, Laura C. *Roommates.* Little.
Smith, Betty. *Tomorrow Will Be Better.* Blakiston.
———. *A Tree Grows in Brooklyn.* Blakiston.
Stolz, Mary. *Ready or Not.* Harper.
Summers, James. *Girl Trouble.* Westminster.
Walker, Mildred. *Winter Wheat.* Harcourt.
Weber, Lenora. *Beany Malone.* Crowell.
Whitney, Phyllis. *Linda's Homecoming.* Crowell.
Wilcox, Don. *Basketball Star.* Little.
Worth, Kathryn. *The Middle Button.* Doubleday.

Informational reading

Allen, Betty and Briggs, Mitchell. *Behave Yourself.* Lippincott.

Bro, Marguerite Harmon. *Let's Talk About You.* Doubleday.

Crow, Alice and Lester D. *Learning to Live with Others.* Heath.

Fedder, Ruth. *A Girl Grows Up.* McGraw.

Fosdick, Harry Emerson. *On Being a Real Person.* Harper.

Giesel, John B. and Spaulding, Francis T. *Personal Problems and Morale.* Houghton.

Ryan, Mildred Graves. *Cues for You.* Appleton.

Strain, Frances Bruce. *Teen Days.* Appleton.[13]

A scope-and-sequence chart of language skills to be taught from Grades 7 through 12 is also included in the Katy guide. As can be seen in the illustrative unit, some grammar as well as other skills is taught in relation to the unit.

Teachers of Junior High School English

The scope of the language-arts program in Grades 7, 8, and 9 can be seen in the special qualities and characteristics expected of English teachers listed in a bulletin on the junior high school published by the Indiana State Department:

> Teachers of the language arts should be competent in all the general qualities peculiar to junior high school teachers and in the following additional areas:
>
> 1. Ability to relate literature to the early adolescent in such a way as to develop interest and enthusiasm for literature.
> 2. Knowledge of the wide range of literature written specifically for children and adolescents, of historical fiction, dramatic writing, contemporary stories of human relations, science, and space.
> 3. Skill in establishing boundaries in activities and discussions within which children feel free to do and say the many things which allow for expression of the borderline thinking that characterizes this age group.
> 4. Ability to assist the junior high school student to extend and refine his vocabulary in order to express his ideas effectively.
> 5. Understanding of our cultural heritage.

---

[13] *Ibid.,* pp. 16–21.

6. Ability to establish, in students, concepts and understandings of subcultures.
7. Ability to develop appreciation for knowledge.
8. Ability to identify pupil needs with reference to skill-building.
9. Ability to teach reading skills as needed.
10. Ability to encourage and foster intellectual curiosity.
11. Ability to correct students in a friendly and effective manner while guiding thoughtful, interesting discussions and writings.
12. Ability to read, speak, and write with an advanced degree of competence.
13. Ability to explain to student, parent, and community groups the aims and outcomes of the program in language arts.
14. Ability to recognize when necessary the assignment of a pupil to remedial work.[14]

It may appear that a paragon rather than a human being is required for the task of teaching English to young adolescents. If this is true, then we are fortunate to have some such paragons in our classrooms. Most junior high schools have at least several English teachers who possess these competencies. A junior high school English teacher should have some special training for his job. The background usually given secondary school English teachers is not sufficient. He should know much about the psychology of twelve- to fifteen-year-olds; he must know how to work with them happily yet firmly. He should have competence in the fields listed above and be able to apply them as suggested. This presents a challenge to institutions engaged in educating English teachers for junior high schools as well as to the teacher himself.

Evaluation of Junior High School English

The Indiana Bulletin expresses a philosophy of evaluation which is applicable to this discussion:

> Any program for evaluating pupil growth should be designed to help the child to improve himself. The communication program is such that much of the work done by the students must be evaluated on standards other than those which can be measured precisely. The beauty of description, the expression of feeling through the use of words, the expression of an idea are exploratory maneuvers of a growing mind in the throes of development which must be nurtured with intellectual care.

---

[14] *The Junior High School, loc. cit.*, p. 26.

The language-arts program is evaluated in terms of specific teaching and learning goals. Measures must be established for ascertaining the progress toward these goals. In many situations in the language arts, the teacher must make a subjective judgment of the student's progress. It is not practicable to reduce learning in the language arts to objective measures if the program is realistic in meeting pupil needs.

. . . The more effective program is the one that involves the student with the teacher in making evaluative judgments. The evaluation program should give emphasis to pupil progress in academic, personal-social, and emotional areas of development. One effective activity for measuring growth develops from having the class as a whole define the purposes of the instructional unit and then having the group assess frequently the growth they are making toward attaining these purposes.[15]

Standardized tests of language competencies and reading ability are often used to assess progress in the secondary school. The following well-known and frequently used tests listed here are examples of the material available: the "Cooperative English Test: Usage, Spelling, and Vocabulary" for Grades 7–16; "Basic Language Skills: Iowa Every-Pupil Tests of Basic Skills, Test C" for Grades 5–9, which yield scores on punctuation, capitalization, usage, spelling, and sentence sense as well as a total language score; the "California Language Test," a subtest of *California Achievement Tests*, which gives scores on mechanics of English and grammar, and spelling, as well as a total score. Many tests of reading ability are also available. Among the more commonly used are the "Sequential Tests of Educational Progress: Reading," commonly referred to as the "Step Tests," the "Iowa Silent Reading Tests: New Edition," and the "Stanford Achievement Test: Reading." As is true of all achievement tests which are general in scope, each of these tests has definite deficiencies. Some are quite reliable in one or two phases, but not too reliable in the rest. Some have quite high validity and reliability in the total score, but cannot be relied upon for the diagnosis of individual skills. Others may include items which modern educators reject as unimportant or even false for present-day curriculums. This weakness occurs most often in items of usage and grammar.

One of the strengths of standardized testing lies in the assistance

---

[15] *Ibid.*, pp. 25–26.

it gives teachers and administrators in evaluating the learning of their school population as compared with that of children of supposedly similar backgrounds. In order for such evaluation to take place, other things must be known about the children and the local curriculum. Are these children comparable in intelligence to those who were used to standardize the test? Are the items selected for the test similar to the materials taught to these children? A still more important value of a standardized testing program lies in the comparison of the scores the same child makes on different forms of the test several years in succession. This enables the teacher and the child himself to see whether or not he is making satisfactory progress in developing language skills. Again, the knowledge of the individual learner's general level of intelligence is important, for the bright child is expected to progress more rapidly than the less gifted child. When scores are properly used, the over-all class level of intelligence is of little concern to the teacher and administrator.

Standardized tests are never relied upon exclusively as evaluators of achievement—nor should they be. The real measure of achievement in language is the child's ability to perform adequately according to his potential and his level of development in the everyday tasks of reading, writing, speaking, and listening. Each performance needs to be evaluated for improvement shown as well as for errors made. Additional tasks and experiences should be assigned to correct inaccurate patterns, reinforce effective language skills, or stimulate further growth. Thus, evaluation should be a part—and often the basis—of the daily learning activities of every student.

Conclusions

The turbulent nature of early adolescence poses certain peculiar problems in furnishing guidance for learning activities in the English classroom. The wide variation in levels of maturity—social and intellectual as well as physical—makes it imperative that the program be flexible both in content and in method. The rapid widening of horizons during this developmental period necessitates a wider vocabulary, more versatility in language use, and greater proficiency in reading. These and other potential benefits make the task of teaching and learning English at this level both challenging and somewhat frightening. So much depends upon the development and

effective use of language skills for growing into maturity success-fully.
This list of goals for a modern program of language arts for Grades 7, 8, and 9 may serve to furnish the scope for this important task:

1. Skill in analyzing and evaluating the spoken word and skill in expressing oneself through speech that evidences a good command of the English language.
2. Skill in listening for the purpose of developing ideas.
3. Skill in organizing ideas and information obtained from reading and listening.
4. Skill in writing sentences, paragraphs, and themes using the accepted techniques of good writing and thereby exhibiting a command of the written English language.
5. Skill in the use of reference sources.
6. Growth in reading skills, tastes, and appreciations.
7. Growth in analyzing one's assumptions by referring to original source materials.
8. Growth in identifying personal values in terms of the culture in which one lives.[16]

---

[16] *Ibid.*, p. 22.

CHAPTER V

English in Grades 10, 11, and 12

Although young people aged sixteen to eighteen are nearing adulthood, they still have developmental needs. Language is as important to this age level as it is to the earlier stages. Personality and language power are still in the process of developing.

Language Education Goals for the Senior High

Since the statement of the Cardinal Principles of Education[1] was published in 1918, as part of a much more extended report on secondary education, curriculum-makers generally have taken the needs and interests of the learner into consideration when planning content and method. These seven principles are: (1) health, (2) command of the fundamental processes of learning, (3) worthy home membership, (4) vocation, (5) citizenship, (6) worthy use of leisure time, and (7) ethical character.

Several modifications of and some additions to the Cardinal Principles have been published by national groups through the years. Much research on adolescent behavior has resulted in strengthening these statements. In 1938 the Educational Policies Commission redefined and brought up to date the general objectives of education. Many courses of study in English are based on the four groups of objectives identified by the Commission:

1. The Objectives of Self-Realization.
2. The Objectives of Human Relationship.
3. The Objectives of Economic Efficiency.
4. The Objectives of Civic Responsibility.[2]

---

[1] Commission on the Reorganization of Secondary Education. *Cardinal Principles of Secondary Education*, U.S. Office of Education Bulletin No. 35 (Washington, D.C.: USGPO, 1918), pp. 11–15.

[2] Educational Policies Commission, National Education Association of the United States and the American Association of School Administrators, *The Purposes of Education in America* (Washington, D.C.: National Education Association, 1938), p. 47.

The National Council of Teachers of English took these categories and expanded them in terms of the language needs of older adolescents in the Council's first curriculum volume, *The English Language Arts.*

1. Wholesome Personal Development.
2. Dynamic and Worthwhile Allegiances through Heightened Moral Perception and a Personal Sense of Values.
3. Growing Intellectual Curiosity and Capacity for Critical Thinking.
4. Effective Use of Language in the Daily Affairs of Life.
5. Habitual and Intelligent Use of the Mass Media of Communication.
6. Growing Personal Interests and Increasingly Mature Standards of Enjoyment.
7. Effective Habits of Work.
8. Competent Use of Language and Reading for Vocational Purposes.
9. Social Sensitivity and Effective Participation in Group Life.
10. Faith in and Allegiance to the Basic Values of a Democratic Society.[3]

Still another refinement of the goals for the language arts in the senior high school is presented in Volume III of the National Council of Teachers of English curriculum series:

1. *Cultivation of Wholesome Personal Living*
   A. Sense of values.
   B. Perspective on oneself and one's time.
   C. Extension of experience so as to be good company *for oneself* as well as good company *for others* through such habits as continued personal reading of high quality and skill in social letter-writing and conversation.
   D. Ability to use the cultural resources in one's community, including the library, radio, television, motion picture, theater, and public platform.
   E. High degree of competence in the basic skills of reading, writing, listening, and speaking.
   F. Intellectual curiosity and creativeness (so far as possible) in all four of the language arts.
   G. Capacity for logical and critical thinking in expression of ideas and in acceptance or rejection of ideas of others.
   H. Personal integrity in thought and expression.

---

[3] Commission on the English Curriculum of The National Council of Teachers of English, *The English Language Arts* (New York: Appleton-Century-Crofts, Inc., © 1952), pp. 41–53. Reprinted by permission of Appleton-Century-Crofts.

I. Intelligent consumption of goods and services because of sensitivity to the denotation and connotation of words; that is, sales resistance without becoming a nuisance as a purchaser; emotional discount for unsubstantiated superlatives in advertisements and sales talks; alert attention to "small print" in contracts, guarantees, and cautions on how to use a product.

2. *Development of Social Sensitivity and Effective Participation in Group Life*
   A. Sensing values in the current scene and their relation to the contributions of past and future.
   B. Recognition of the dignity and worth of every individual.
   C. Control of one's prejudices so as to avoid giving offense or blocking important group action.
   D. Skill in the language arts of persuasion, cooperative planning, discussion, and decision.
   E. Recognition of the social and psychological factors involved in communication with people of different backgrounds.
   F. A sense of responsibility for critical (as well as imaginative) reading and listening in order to understand and appreciate elements in American culture and in that of other nations.

3. *Linguistic Competence Necessary for Vocational Efficiency*
   A. Following and giving directions.
   B. Keeping up with technical knowledge in one's occupation.
   C. Maintaining effective interpersonal relationships: employer-employee, employee-employee, employer-public, employee-public.
   D. Developing needed skills in business letter-writing, in persuasion and exposition, and in techniques of interviewing.[4]

Characteristics of Older Adolescents Which Relate to Language Teaching

Variety of potentials and levels of development. Although nearly all adolescents in the senior high school have begun to mature physically, they do so at different rates. The girls are still ahead of the boys in maturation level, and this is generally noticeable at least into the eleventh grade. The girls are generally more verbal; they talk more and write better than most boys their age. Gradually, however, the gap begins to close and by the time they are ready to graduate, most of the boys will have caught up with the girls in physical,

[4] Commission on the English Curriculum of The National Council of Teachers of English, *The English Language Arts in the Secondary School* (New York: Appleton-Century-Crofts, Inc., © 1956), pp. 44–45. Reprinted by permission of Appleton-Century-Crofts.

social, and verbal development. The results of the Scholastic Aptitude Tests bear this out. There is then more difference among individuals than there is between the sexes.

It is not uncommon to find a reading range from the sixth (or lower) to the fourteenth grades in a typical cross section of sixteen-year-olds. A small percentage have developed the ability to write clearly and effectively, but many still write only with difficulty. Some of these slower learners probably have powers that are undeveloped, while others lack the innate ability to progress very far up the ladder.

Individuals exhibit a wide range of ability in various aspects of language power. The same individual may be very proficient in reading and writing, for example, and quite ineffective in speaking or in spelling and punctuation.

Physical changes affecting language. Young people in their later teens are becoming more accustomed to their mature bodies and to their increased sexual drives. But many are still apprehensive and bewildered. Holden Caulfield in *Catcher in the Rye* is more pathetic than comic in his search for answers about sex and other human relationships, but he is not atypical of many boys between fifteen and twenty.

While they are coming to terms with themselves as adults physically and emotionally, young people need the guidance of sympathetic adults. They need help in extending their vocabularies and their modes of communication. Both sexes often turn to literature to shed light on their problems and to bolster their ideals. Boys seek physically vigorous and morally courageous heroes, while girls prefer romance in which the heroines either solve their problems or meet defeat with their nobility of purpose untarnished.

Strong group identification. The one thing adolescents cannot tolerate is to be isolated from the peer group. In the American culture, not to be one of a crowd or gang is to be an outcast, a misfit, and a miserable human being. As a consequence, young people cooperate on group projects; they are willing to use their talents for the group; and they succumb readily to peer-group pressures.

So much social pressure develops during this period that for most young people the mores of the crowd become a personal behavior code. What the crowd deems important takes precedence over everything else, including school. As a result, the activities suggested or required by the English teacher must be meaningful to the student if they are to compete successfully for his attention and effort as well as for his out-of-school time. Such assignments need not be trivial or nonintellectual in order to have meaning for the adolescent. Many young people are seeking answers to important questions: How does one know if she is ready for marriage? Is there a God? How do you know what is right? How can I be a happy person? What do I want to do to make a living? The English curriculum is filled with literary works dealing with at least some of these questions. Opportunities to read, write, and talk about such subjects will serve to further communication skills. The ability to think critically will be increased if proper learning guidance is given when meaningful opinions are shared and if objective evaluations and understandings are sought. Through such activities, the group's hold on the individual may be loosened. This loosening process assists the thinking adolescent to mature more rapidly and allows him to exert his own individuality.

Feelings of insecurity. Indifference or boredom, rowdyism, or exhibitionism is often a cover-up for deep feelings of insecurity in later adolescence. Adolescents are often overly sensitive and shy but, to avoid ridicule and more hurt, they put on a bold or bored front. Much of their obnoxious behavior—obnoxious, that is, from the adult standpoint—is an attention-getting mechanism. Loud talking, giggling, overly loud laughter, swearing, and considerable use of slang are all devices to attract the attention of adults and to demonstrate acceptance by the peer group, as well as to furnish outlets for their emotions.

The English teacher must be able to recognize these defense mechanisms for what they are and not for what they appear to be. Such outlets as dramatics and role-playing, choral reading, or creative writing will often furnish young people with the positive action they crave and can accept. At the same time, they are learning verbal skills of real importance.

Independence from adults. In American culture the drive for independence begins early, much earlier and more vigorously than in many other cultures. By the time the typical young person has reached the senior high school, he has cut or visibly frayed the parental apron strings. This does not mean that he is a free agent, but he likes to think he is. Most young people need the mature and wise counsel of adults, but they want to be free to seek it out themselves and, above all, they do not want to be told everything: they are willing and eager to search out answers for themselves. Careful but sympathetic guidance by the English teacher is needed to help young people form sound judgments and to make their own choices. The teacher must also be able to show young people their responsibilities for what they say and write.

Choices concerning vocations and marriage are two very important decisions facing older adolescents as they gain independence. These are real concerns that occupy much of their attention during senior high school. Through their dawning realization of the importance of success in a vocation, many young people can be led to the necessity of improving and refining their language skills to meet adult standards. According to several surveys, a relatively high level of English language competency is one of the leading factors in vocational success.

Ideals, values, and aesthetics as related to language. High school students are the most idealistic group in our culture. Although they may not talk about it openly, they are often confused by the varying standards of values they see around them. They are searching, often desperately, for some purpose in life—an identity for themselves and a workable system of ethical and spiritual values. English literature is full of poems, novels, essays, and dramas that deal with values and the beliefs men hold. Young people need help in ferreting out the relevant ideas of these authors. They also need an opportunity to express their doubts and fears in a permissive atmosphere, either in writing or in oral discussions.

Many young people begin to be conscious of the beauty and wonder of the world around them. Some turn to poetry, others to drama, and still others to fine prose to find beautiful expressions of feelings and ideas which they cannot yet verbalize. Many will experiment with words to see whether they can create something of beauty. These are real challenges to the senior high school English teacher.

The Senior High School English Curriculum

Two patterns predominate in the English curriculum of Grades 10, 11, and 12: the separate-subjects approach and the broad-fields or fused approach. It would be difficult to say which of these two patterns occurs more often. Jewett intimates in his report, *English Language Arts in American High Schools,*[5] that the broad-fields approach has become the more important of the two curricular patterns. But this would be difficult to prove with the information at hand.

Separate-subjects curriculum. Many senior high schools divide the English curriculum into discrete segments or subjects. One rather common practice is to devote one semester to composition and grammar and one to literature during each of the three years of high school English. The elements of traditional grammar are taught intensively, with attention to composition skills, outlining, and punctuation. The semesters devoted to literature may be given over to an intensive study of the various literary forms—biography, poetry, drama, the essay, the short story, and the novel—by reading and discussing in detail the standard selections found in most high school anthologies. There is little or no attempt to relate the material of one semester to that of another.

Elective courses in speech, drama, creative writing, business English, or journalism are offered in most large metropolitan high schools. Sometimes students with special abilities or a demonstrated proficiency in language skills may substitute one of these electives for regular English courses. In other schools these courses may be taken in addition to the regular English curriculum.

Fused programs of English. Another system of organization involves the relation of all the aspects of English; this system is often referred to as fusion. Under this arrangement a number of different plans will be found in operation. One plan is to organize the literature in chronological order, by country. World literature may be the focal point for the sophomore year; American literature, for the junior; and English literature for the senior. Instruction in the mechanics of language—usage, grammar, and composition—is fused with the study of literature or taught as short blocks of lessons between the periods devoted to literature.

Another way of organizing the fused program is to build it around literary forms or selected standard works. A third way is to organize the material around thematic units.

---

[5] Arno Jewett, *English Language Arts in American High Schools,* U.S. Office of Education Bulletin No. 13 (Washington, D.C.: USGPO, 1958).

The core curriculum. Very few senior high schools use the core curriculum. At this point in the history of American public education, more and more emphasis is being put on academic excellence in each of the separate disciplines. It is no longer popular to attempt to meet the needs of adolescents by attacking problems which cut across various fields of knowledge. Only occasionally does one find teachers working in tandem or in a modified team arrangement—correlating English and history, for example. In these situations the cooperation between the two fields is more likely to be for the purpose of teaching slow-learning groups (the aim is to make the content of both areas more meaningful by relating one to the other). Another attempt to develop some interrelationship among subject areas is coming from quite another source. Some scholars, who are especially concerned about what the humanities can and should contribute to man through his education, are attempting to revive a genuine interest in the humanities at the high school level as well as at the college level. The *Encyclopaedia Britannica* film series on the humanities is a specific illustration of this more recent trend.

A new synthesis of subject matter is developing within English, as well as in mathematics and other disciplines. A "New English" is evolving, much as the "New Math" evolved in the past decade. No strong pattern has yet developed, but a return to English as English —at least in most of the high schools of the nation—seems to be the present trend.

Scope and Sequence in the Language Arts

In many school systems there is a continuous program in the language arts in Grades 7–12 or even K–12. The same goals form the basis of the total program at all levels. The details of the specific content and the specific methods used are adjusted to the level and needs of young people as they progress up the educational ladder, but the basic pattern of organization remains the same. Thus much of the general discussion concerning the junior high school is applicable here also.

In many senior high schools, scope-and-sequence charts are used to designate the basic language skills to be taught at each level. When used flexibly, these charts can have real value. They assign responsibility for introducing and teaching certain major skills and concepts. This gives some semblance of order to the sequence. Without this kind of guide, the teacher too frequently feels he has the sole responsibility for teaching almost everything anew each year. The sequence charts help to prevent repetition of the same material year after year. They also insure that no important points are overlooked altogether. They provide for a reasonable amount of consideration of the reading, writing, speaking, and listening skills of students as they progress from level to level. The interrelatedness of the language areas is readily seen in these charts.

The Denver language-arts guide has charts for language, reading, writing, speaking, and listening for each major level of development. For example, the Listening Chart for Senior High School is divided into nine major areas of activities with "Process or Skill" and "Expected Attainment" listed under each.

I. *Incidental Instruction*
Process or Skill
Assignments.
Suggestions for preparation of specific lessons.
Supplemental information.
Expected Attainment
Attentive listening: awareness that incidental directions will not usually be repeated.
Awareness of such causes of ineffective listening as chattering with neighbors, daydreaming, indifference, worry, fatigue, general inattentiveness; conscious efforts to eliminate causes of poor listening.
Feeling of freedom in asking questions to clarify understanding.
Selection of items in assignments, suggestions, and the like that have personal meaning and pertinence to a particular purpose.[6]

The eight other areas are: "Incidental Recitation," "Prepared Recitation," "Discussion," "Conversation," "Literature," "Dramatic Activities," "Public Speeches," "Radio, Television."[7]

Unit Teaching

In addition to these scope-and-sequence charts, the Denver guide includes a sample thematic unit for each grade level. The eleventh-

---

[6] *A Program in English: A Guide for Teaching the Language Arts; Kindergarten through Grade Twelve* (Denver: The Department of Instruction, 1953), p. 307.
[7] *Ibid.*, pp. 301–11.

grade unit is entitled "American Literature: The Regions of America." Themes for the remaining units also center around America, with three divisions—*Life, Liberty,* and *The Pursuit of Happiness*—serving as focal points.

The first section, *Life,* deals with such topics as "Regional Literature," "Racial Problems," "Lives of Famous Americans," and "Religion and Philosophy." *Liberty* treats of "Colonial Beginnings," "Historic Documents," "Literature of the War Years," and "The Spirit of Democracy." Under *Pursuit of Happiness* are found "Humor," "Adventure," "The Out-of-Doors," "Types of Literature," "Understanding People," and "The Fine Arts."[8]

Some school systems use the thematic units for at least part of their senior high school English programs. Some of these units often deal with a particular literary form or a specific selection, such as *Julius Caesar, A Tale of Two Cities,* "Reading Poetry for Enjoyment," or "Understanding the Drama." The Minnesota guide[9] assigns "Poetry for Everyone" to the tenth grade and "Drama" to the twelfth grade. It also includes some language-centered units such as "The Power of Language" and "Reading Magazines for Pleasure and Profit" for tenth grade, "The Role of the Press" for eleventh grade, and "What Shall I Read?" for twelfth grade. The rest of the units are centered on social or individual problems such as "Family and Home" and "Team Play and Individuality" for the tenth grade, "The Search for the Good Life in America" for eleventh grade, and "Understanding the World at Work," "The Influence of Environment on Personality Through Literature," and "Developing a Personal Philosophy" for twelfth grade.

Units for senior high school English are organized in the same general manner as they are for junior high school. Following are excerpts from a resource unit for eleventh-grade English, written and used by the English teachers of Katy, Texas. This material will illustrate how literature, writing, grammar, critical thinking, listening, and speaking are all related through the unit theme:

---

[8] *Ibid.,* p. 153.
[9] *A Guide to Instruction in the Language Arts,* Curriculum Bulletin No. 18 (St. Paul: State of Minnesota Department of Public Instruction, 1956), p. 6.

A Sense of Values

I. *Objectives*

  A. Knowledge, concepts, attitudes:

    To recognize the stated and implied values in what one reads, hears, and observes.

    To evaluate the merits of these stated and implied values.

    To analyze and evaluate one's own values.

    To realize that values are not the same for all.

    To consider the relative worth of material and non-material possessions.

    To understand the forces which mold our attitudes, ideals, and values (such as environment, education, personal abilities, and experiences).

    To realize that the inspiration which can be found in idealistic literature can be used in our own lives.

  B. Skills:

    To evaluate critically books and magazine articles which express attitudes toward life.

    To read idealistic literature with understanding and enjoyment.

    To read poetry with the definite purpose of seeking values implied and expressed there.

    To express effectively in writing one's own ideals and attitudes toward life.

    To express and maintain a point of view in writing.

    To use details to support general statements.

    To participate in a panel or group discussion with ease.

    To write an imaginary conversation in collaboration with another student based on characters from reading.

    To read a selection orally so that it is enjoyable to others.

II. *Suggested Activities*

  A. Initiatory:

    Read to the class such poems as Edna St. Vincent Millay's "God's World," Sara Teasdale's "Barter," and Edwin Arlington Robinson's "Richard Cory" and "Miniver Cheevy." Following readings with discussion: What do Teasdale and Millay consider important in life? What did Miniver Cheevy and Richard Cory have in life? What did each lack? What was the result of this? What is important to you in life? Ask the students to list on a sheet of paper three wishes they would like to have fulfilled. Keep these papers until the completion of the unit to see if there have been any changes in ideas.

B. Developmental:

Tell the class what some of the people you know in books or in real life valued. Call attention to the fact that there is great variation in their ideas—that most of us value the same things to some extent but some more than others. Illustrate on the chalkboard a *rating of values* in which the things we value might be listed in the order of their importance to us. Discuss some of the forces which determine our values, such as environment, education, personal abilities, and experiences. Which values reflect the fact that we are Americans? Are Americans materialistic? Why might we seem so to other people?

State that American writers have had much to say about values. Present a bibliography for individual reading of books which deal with what is important in life. Have these books in the classroom and have students select a book to read. Give the students the remainder of the class period to read, checking on the suitability of their choices and making further recommendations as needed. Reports on individual reading may be given individually, in groups according to type of book, or in a class discussion. Such questions as the following may be used:

What is an important value which the author sets forth in the book?

In what way does he bring out the value?

Discuss the merits of the value, giving grounds for your reaction.

Pair students according to books they have read and have them work out together an imaginary conversation between characters in their books. For example, the characters could compare their ideas on such subjects as education or medicine. Jesse Stuart in *The Thread That Runs So True* could talk with Miss Dove in *Good Morning, Miss Dove* or Martin Arrowsmith could talk with Dr. Zhivago. Have these conversations recorded on the tape recorder and played back for the class.

Assign the reading in common of short poems and prose selections to help the students become aware of what to read for and to aid the student in his thinking. Selections are listed under *Suggested Materials.* Consult *Teacher's Manual* for questions for discussion.

Let each student select a passage of poetry or prose, to read aloud to the class, which represents his values. Have him point out the values. List these on the board and have the class cooperatively work out a scale of values, putting the most important or those most frequently mentioned at the top.

Have each student write a short paper in which he tells some interesting experience he had which involved no money. Read or have read the best papers in class.

Discuss what we mean by living a "good life." Plan a panel discussion based upon the following questions: How do newspapers and magazines assist the reading public in its search for the "good life"? Bring articles to illustrate and evaluate.

What do radio and television do to help the public to find the "good life"? What broadcasts of drama, music, and other types of programs contribute? Listen to programs which report on American ideas and ideals, such as "Omnibus," "Youth Wants to Know," "The Twentieth Century," and "University Forum," and evaluate these ideas. Such popular programs as "Father Knows Best," "The Loretta Young Show," "Kraft Theater," "Wagon Train," and "Playhouse 90" might furnish material for discussion along this line also.

How are motion pictures related to the search for the "good life" in America? Students might discuss the following questions, using particular pictures which they have seen for concrete examples to support their opinions:

If one were to judge entirely by motion pictures, what do Americans value most in life?

According to the movies, what kind of people are most admired?

How do movies represent American family life?

What false impressions of American life might foreigners get if they depended on motion pictures for their understanding?

Can you give an example of a motion picture which truthfully represents the "good life" in America? What ideals, goals, pleasures, or philosophy in general does it show?

On the whole do movies present a true picture of American life and ideals?

C. Culminating:

Have the students write a paper on their attitude toward life, pointing out any challenges to their thinking which they have experienced during the course of the unit. Here they may refer to their three wishes listed at the beginning of the unit.

Check students' charts and papers for evidence of need

for reviewing usage problems, especially pointing out
needs for reviewing usage of modifiers, plurals of nouns,
prepositions, and conjunctions. Use material as needed
from Tressler, *"Using Modifiers, Nouns, and Joining
Words."* . . .
Find examples of sentences which need improvement.
Show the students these examples and discuss how they
may be improved by using all of the methods taught
during the year.

III. *Suggested Evaluation*

Give short-answer and essay tests on the literary selections
and on ideas brought up for discussion in class to evaluate
ability to read with understanding and appreciate literature
dealing with ideas and ideals.

Use a poem not studied during the unit to test ability to
read poetry for the truth or ideals expressed.

Use discussions and panels to check ability to express ideas
and ideals and to support them by reference to personal
experience, observation, reading, or listening.

Use all written composition, including subjective tests, to
check ability to organize and to express and develop ideas.

Check written work for growth in sentence structure, spelling, capitalization, and punctuation developed in this and
previous units.[9]

Although many authorities in English education, as well as the
Curriculum Commission of the National Council of Teachers of
English favor, the thematic units with some attention to literary
forms and special language problems in the senior high school, it
would be erroneous to surmise that most of the programs of English
at that level are so organized. Jewett found that only a relatively
small number of courses of study for senior high school English
used the thematic-unit approach—a much smaller group than at the
junior high school level. Jewett concludes:

Most English programs in Grades 10 and 11 have a multitype organization. A few units may be organized according to literary type, a
few according to theme, a few according to communication need.
The more traditional courses may also offer topical units in grammar and usage. After examining the courses of study for Grades
10, 11, and 12, one may safely conclude that a much more traditional type of program prevails in the senior high than in the junior
high years.[10]

---

[9] *A Resource Guide for English Language Arts,* Grades 11 and 12 (Katy,
Texas: 1959), pp. 63–72.
[10] Jewett, *op. cit.,* p. 65.

Without a doubt, the most common kind of organization of English programs in the senior high school is by types of literature —biography, essay, novel, drama, short story, and poetry—interspersed with sessions on language skills and problems.

The eleventh-grade programs quite generally focus on American literature. This course is most frequently organized according to types of literature by American authors although the chronological and regional approaches are also used in many schools.

The twelfth-grade English program shows the greatest diversity of approaches. Only sixteen states require twelfth-grade English for graduation from high school, although many of the others encourage it. Most high schools offer a course in twelfth-grade English; and the larger ones offer a variety of electives (see Chapter II), every approach being used, and it is almost impossible to distinguish a dominant pattern.

The tenth-grade programs do not have the uniformity of approach typical of the eleventh grade, but neither are they so diversified as those of the twelfth. The literary-forms approach predominates, and thematic units centering around concerns of youth are also popular. Multitype organization is the outstanding characteristic of these programs.

Some schools are attempting to meet the wide range of levels in language among older adolescents through special groupings (see Chapter III). Three groupings are most common: superior—honors classes, "great works" courses, special writing courses; average—programs discussed earlier in this chapter; and remedial—special reading classes, special help in writing and in grammar. The San Diego, California, city school system[11] has a separate guide for each of the three ability levels. There is no attempt made to achieve any unity between the levels. For example, the twelfth-grade honors course designed for the college-bound students consists of depth reading in English and world literature as well as extensive work on writing. The plans for the middle or average group include a study of literature by types. The program for the lower one third or the noncollege-bound students consists of thematic units. Diversity in programs indeed appears to be the order of the day.

---

[11] *A Guide for Teaching English, Grade XII; A Guide for Teaching Contemporary Literature, Grade XII; A Guide for Teaching English Literature (Including References for World Literature) Grade XII* (San Diego, California: San Diego Public Schools, 1958 and 1960).

Teaching Composition in Grades 10, 11, and 12

Most young people as well as adults feel that writing is difficult. Frequently what they think they know cannot be captured on paper. Many adults avoid situations where written composition is required because they feel that they cannot express themselves adequately in writing. Yet many of these adults have graduated from high school, where they have had a minimum of three years of English, to say nothing of those who have also had twelfth-grade English as well as freshman composition in college. Writing is always a part of any English curriculum. Where does the problem lie?

Unfortunately, in the past some schools have placed so much stress on the other aspects of language—such as grammar, usage, and literature—that little time was left for writing. Although some high schools have long stressed writing in their English programs, the amount of writing actually done was kept to a minimum—perhaps because a teacher with 150 to 175 students simply does not have the time to read and correct many papers from each student.

Some schools have experimented with the use of lay readers for reading and grading themes. Lay readers are generally women who are college graduates, English majors who want part-time work which can be done at home. A training program is set up for these readers to help them learn what to look for in themes and what kinds of comments to make on papers. Specific conferences with the teacher are also required to enable the reader to understand the purpose for specific assignments and to convey her reactions to the papers. Themes are turned over to the lay reader for reading and grading and returned to the teacher for further work with the students. Although much enthusiasm has been expressed for this plan by some of the teachers who have worked with lay readers, there is still skepticism among others.

The recommendation which has grown out of both the Conant Report and that of the National Council of Teachers of English is to reduce the English teacher's load to a maximum of 100 students. A few schools have already acted on this suggestion. Usually in these cases more stress is placed on writing, both quantitatively and qualitatively, because the teacher has more time to direct the individual's efforts and to criticize them effectively.

There has been much talk but little productive research on what kinds of instruction produce effective writers. No conclusive evidence is available to prove that the more one writes the better one writes, although this has become a rather popular theory. Several interesting studies conducted recently suggest that perhaps what one reads may have as much or more effect on the quality of the writing one later produces. More carefully controlled research is needed in this area to determine the effects of certain kinds of writing assignments, as well as those of the quantity of writing, on various kinds of students. Although no one who has studied the problem of producing writing ability in young people believes this can be accomplished without requiring—or at least stimulating—much writing, this is obviously not the whole answer.

The kind of writing required of students is another area which needs much investigation. Does it matter whether the writing is of a personal nature—expressions of feelings or emotions, outpourings of personal experiences or concerns, imaginative writing—or of an impersonal, objective nature—statements of opinion, presentations of facts, analyses of someone else's ideas? At present, this question is a focal point of argument among teachers and educators who believe they know all about writing. Many teachers encourage both kinds of writing. They use the personal approach to free the young person—to make him aware that he does have something to say and that he can write so that others want to read it. After the young person acquires some self-confidence, he can be introduced slowly but surely to the rigorous discipline of more objective writing and good exposition.

Another factor in producing effective writers, which needs research, is the effectiveness of teacher criticism as compared with peer criticism. For years people like Lou La Brant and Dora V. Smith have advocated that the teacher's judgment was not enough, that the writer deserves a wider audience and a critical one. They also believe that this critical sharing and reacting to one another's work is one of the chief catalysts in the improvement of content, organization, and the mechanics of writing. It is a truism to say that there is need for much more genuine investigation of what constitutes effective teaching of writing.

Reading Guidance

For years one of the objectives of high school English programs has been to make readers of young people, to encourage them to read widely, and to improve their tastes in reading. The universal acceptance of the book report attests to this objective.

Unfortunately, according to a number of research studies, the time-honored book-reporting system has not been entirely successful. For example, "A recent Gallup poll found 39 per cent of the college-trained were reading some books, while only 19 per cent of those with high school educations . . . were reading books."[12] Apparently the book-reporting system has not produced readers.

One of the possible reasons for this failure is that the books required for reports were frequently not those which many young people would choose to read on their own. The list often consisted of books that the teacher thought worthwhile or books that were considered classics.

Another possible reason is that the very act of reporting was dull and uninteresting rather than stimulating and motivating. Many young people worked harder at escaping reading than at enjoying reading. They used "classic comics," synopses on book jackets, or the knowledge of friends to substitute for reading—and with reasonable success. This did not promote a love of books but, rather, set up an antipathy for literature. Of course, there were some who benefited from the practice, but most of these young people would probably have read anyway.

How can this avoidance of reading be overcome? Educators believe strongly that continual reading of books and the best periodicals is important for the mature adult. Reading is a method by which one gains additional knowledge, learns about oneself and others, lives vicariously, and builds deeper understandings and appreciation for the world around him.

Authorities generally hold that if the teacher or librarian appeals to the interests and needs of adolescents through books—if the young person has an opportunity to share informally his enthusi-

---

[12] Jean D. Grambs, *The Development of Lifetime Reading Habits: A Report of a Conference Called by the Committee on Reading Development in New York, June 25–26, 1954.* Published for the National Book Committee by R. R. Bowker. pp. iv–v.

asms for what he reads—he is more apt to develop a genuine enthusiasm for reading. He will come to realize that books have much to offer in the way of information or even of escape from reality.

Helping the young person find the right book at the right time is an art every English teacher must cultivate. Effective reading guidance must be based upon a wide knowledge of books young people generally like and a thorough knowledge of young people and their reactions. Given these two qualities, the teacher is usually much more successful in helping young people discover books they did not know they wanted and which bring them satisfaction as well as books which they are certain they will enjoy.

The teacher must also allow adolescents to react freely and honestly to what they read. He must avoid the tendency to tell them what they *should* think, how they *should* feel. Only by gaining confidence in their own ability to react to the printed page will young people develop a liking and a taste for good books.

Students in the senior high school should be given ample opportunity to read widely under the guidance of competent teachers and librarians. This means that time must be set aside for guided free reading, for trips to the library, for enthusiastic sharing. This means that the teacher must also read widely in order to keep up with new works and build backgrounds in the old, established literature for young people. An abundance of high-quality new material with real appeal for adolescents is being published weekly. There is much from the past with which the English teacher should be familiar. The teacher's task is not to compare the merits of the old with those of the new but, rather, to become familiar with a wide range of good books which young people will find satisfying.

If young people are to become mature readers after they leave school, they must be encouraged to read good books in their high school years. So many things compete for young people's time that what we offer them in school must have real meaning and satisfaction for them.

Conclusion

More than 50 per cent of those who graduate from high school now go on to college. Success in college calls for a high degree of verbal ability. Even for the remaining 50 per cent—those who become housewives or enter the business and industrial world, communication is important to both success and happiness. All English teachers—but especially those teaching in Grades 10, 11, and 12 —have a great responsibility to help each young person to develop in all aspects of language power to the performance level of which he is capable. This is a frightening prospect, but a challenging one.

CHAPTER VI

Special Problems and Trends in the Teaching of English

Recently the term the *"New English"* has been seen in newspaper and periodical. It refers to changes proposed in the curriculum of the secondary school. As yet, it is a nebulous term; its precise meaning depends upon the situation to which the writer refers. English, as a subject discipline, is in a state of ferment—as is nearly every other subject field commonly taught in the secondary schools and colleges of America. This ferment arises in part from the new knowledge which is being produced by scholars, as well as from the reorganization and re-evaluation of much which has been traditionally incorporated in the English curriculum. No doubt the next decade will be one of controversy, experimentation, and much change in the specific content and method in secondary English teaching. It is to be hoped that this change and experimentation will result in progress toward more effective learning of skills and a greater appreciation of language, which is basic to our humanness and to the acquisition of further knowledge and effectiveness in all other areas of life.

Special Problems and Trends

Literature. For years the controversy has raged between English teachers who feel that the only literature worth reading in high school is the "classics," and those who believe that contemporary literature should be used almost exclusively. Defensible arguments are posed on both sides.

The conservatives want to be sure that a work has literary merit and lasting value before school time is taken to study it. They believe that the test of time is of the utmost importance in determining these values. They also say that, unless young people are helped to understand the structure of our various forms of literature, they will often lose much in the reading of serious drama, poetry, and prose.

A study of some of the finest examples of each literary form is the best way to instill a genuine appreciation of literature in young people. Literature is art and art has form; in order to appreciate literature as art, its form must be understood.

The modernists point out that much of our best literature—the real classics—is concerned with subjects and themes which are beyond the scope or experience of adolescents. Unless the reader has some background—direct or vicarious—to bring to the content of the book, he will be unable to understand what the writer is saying and will often come away with misconceptions of the author's purpose or theme. For example, high school students who read Hawthorne's *The Scarlet Letter* frequently come away with the impression that Hawthorne is writing about adultery, thus missing his significant theme by a wide margin. The average American adolescent has little knowledge of the life and theological thinking of the Puritans, and little more on the effects of sin on the personality and character of different types of individuals.

Literature, in addition to being fine writing, should have something to say to the reader which he can understand. Contemporary writers more frequently write about themes which adolescents understand and which relate to experiences with which young people are familiar. Literature chosen for young people should be based on their needs and interests. If they read primarily what they find difficult and almost incomprehensible, they will not develop a taste for good literature. But if they are offered materials which they can comprehend and enjoy reading, they will learn to like reading and will go on to discover the classics when they have more experience. Rosenblatt stated this position very aptly when she said: "Those who cram the classics down the students' throats long before they are ready are careless of the fate of the great works of the past."[1]

Neither of these positions tells the whole story. Each has its merits and its weaknesses. The present trend in the secondary school is to consider the dominant needs and interests of the adolescents and to search for selections of literary merit which deal with these factors, striking a balance between the modern and the classical. The anthologies used as literature textbooks in nearly all secondary school English classes are all organized on that basis to a greater or lesser

---

[1] Louise Rosenblatt, *Literature as Exploration* (New York: Appleton-Century-Crofts, Inc., 1938), p. 257.

degree. Some of the writings of Shakespeare, some of the outstanding British and American poets, some of the outstanding essayists and philosophers will no doubt continue to be read by adolescents in their English classes. The selection of novels, short stories, and modern poetry and drama, however, will be more diversified than in the past. Many schools are choosing novels like *The Yearling* or *The Red Badge of Courage* to replace *Silas Marner*. *John Brown's Body* often replaces *Idylls of the King* and the poetry of Dylan Thomas or T. S. Eliot is substituted for that of Wordsworth or Tennyson.

Another trend in the teaching of literature is to reduce the amount of time spent in reading and studying a single selection, such as *Julius Caesar* or *Macbeth*. Greater attention is paid to the text of the play or selection, and less attention to the history of the Shakespearean theater or the Elizabethan Period. A more intensive study of the selection as literature illuminates general aspects of style and literary criticism, such as theme, character portrayal, and symbols.

Along with this short, intensive study of specific selections, much emphasis is also being placed on extensive reading of similar kinds of materials. The student is allowed to choose from among a variety of selections those in which he is most interested and which he is most likely to comprehend and enjoy. This procedure helps the individual learn to choose his own reading more wisely and with discrimination from the quantity of works available. This is important if he is to become an independent, discriminating reader as an adult.

More attention is being paid to teaching the reading skills necessary for a better understanding of the different kinds of literature. Nearly every textbook on reading in the secondary school or on the methods of teaching English in the high school has a section devoted to reading skills. For example, Burton, in his *Literature Study in the High School,* says: "Mature reading of biography demands two major skills: skill in following various patterns of organization, and skill in critical evaluation."[2] He breaks down each of these skills into several discrete parts. For patterns of organization he suggests "key episodes" and "various influences on the life and work of the subject" as two elements with which students should be familiar. Under critical evaluation he lists "authenticity" and "biographer's relation-

[2] Dwight L. Burton, *Literature Study in the High School,* rev. ed. (New York: Holt, Rinehart & Winston, Inc., 1964), p. 189.

ship to the subject" as two essentials. Other skills for reading poetry, essays, and drama are also discussed.

The structure of the selection as it relates to the theme—symbolism, literary devices, foreshadowing—are also being stressed in the senior high school. The trend is thus toward wide reading and the development of skills and understandings that will enable students to read with greater depth and insight.

Writing. Written composition has always been a major concern of the English teacher. Many methods have been tried, but there appears to be no magic formula that works for all teachers or students. In recent years more emphasis on written communication has been urged by business and industry as well as by colleges. There is more and more need for people to communicate their ideas in written form through reports, proposals, research plans, employee complaints, and the like. The clear expression of ideas is made possible by effective organization, clear purpose, and careful word choice. These skills can be mastered at least to a degree, by all secondary school students. The problem remains as to how best to accomplish this.

Several factors concerning the teaching of written composition are fairly well agreed upon. Critical thinking is both a prerequisite to and a result of effective writing. Attention given to the elements of critical thinking in reading or listening will assist the individual in evaluating his own ideas. Young people are apt to jump to conclusions, to accept as truth what is written in a magazine or a book or heard from the platform or the television set. They too frequently feel that, because it appears in black and white or is transmitted from a television studio, it is *ipso facto* authoritative and right. Much emphasis needs to be placed on critical thinking in every English course as well as in other courses in the school.

Opportunity to write frequently and to have that writing critically evaluated by both peers and teacher is necessary for development in all types of written composition. Learning about sentence structure, grammar, and punctuation may be important, but it will not substitute for writing. Filling in blanks or identifying incomplete sentences in workbooks will not suffice. Few young people have difficulty identifying incomplete or runon sentences when these are presented as isolated examples. It is the difficulty of sorting ideas into separate yet related sentences when composing that causes the trouble. Only by much meaningful practice in composition does the student begin to gain mastery over sentence structure and the mechanics of writing.

The third factor is that the writer must have something to say; he must know something about his subject before he can communicate. This requires some interest in, and experience with, the subject. The experience may be vicarious—that is, gained through reading or watching television programs—but it must be real and effective. Too frequently English teachers have tended to assign composition subjects similar to those which they themselves were assigned in college—subjects such as "The Life of Poe as Related to His Poetry" or "The Elements of Tragedy in Macbeth." They forget that they were not only older, and thus more experienced, than their high school students, but also guided—through reading and research—to the necessary background information. If young high school students are allowed to write about things with which they are familiar and about which they have some real concern, they will learn more about the skills of composition and effective writing than if they have to struggle with these skills while dealing with new concepts and information that do not greatly interest them.

One authority on teaching composition asserts that if a student can write clear and explicit instructions on, for example, how to start a car on a cold morning, and if by applying the instructions the teacher is able to start his car, that student deserves a respectable grade in composition. He may not be able to write on a literary subject with any degree of effectiveness unless and until the literature reaches him "down where he lives." Then he can react intelligently and write with some clarity because he has something to say. If and when he has something to say and he feels what he writes will make a difference to someone he respects, he will usually be willing to revise and correct his work until it is structurally and mechanically sound and accurate.

Other factors are less well established, but several should be mentioned. Some teachers have found that they have more success in teaching writing when they allow a student to write on any subject of his choice in any manner he chooses. This often stimulates students who otherwise are convinced that they cannot write. Once they feel reasonably successful with this medium, they are able to learn composition skills more readily because they can see some use for them. Another debatable point is whether the skills should be taught first, step by step, with practice provided for one skill at a time—writing topic sentences, writing a paragraph which will show development by illustration, studying the rules for use of the comma or the semicolon, identifying phrases and clauses, or using quotation marks—or whether young people should have much experience of composing first, then learn the skills which will make their writing more effective. These two positions represent very different concepts of the way effective writing is learned. The first one maintains that writing is made up of a series of discrete skills which can be taught in sequence and which, when learned, will produce effective writing. The other position holds that writing is an expression of the individual personality and must have unity with the individual. According to this view, the skills are merely rules or helpful suggestions which man applies to his writing but which vary with the nature and purpose of the writing. Different points of view as to how language control is developed are represented here. The first group believes that the whole is made up of its parts put together in logical sequence—that by learning all there is to know about the mechanics of composition, an individual can then write in a reasonably accurate and coherent manner. The other group believes that a composition must have a purpose and must show that purpose through unity. If after attempting to say something of importance on paper, the writer discovers through reader reaction that he has not communicated his ideas effectively, he will then be in a position to understand what the rules mean and why they are important. The former position is held more widely, but there is little evidence to support either position except subjective personal experience. Research is needed in this area.

Listening. Twenty-five years ago listening was not a recognized part of the language-arts program. Today the majority of secondary English courses include the teaching of listening. The rise in the use of oral mass media in our daily lives has made listening increasingly important as an information-getting device or learning tool.

A few studies have been made to ascertain what elements of listening can best be taught and to devise some methods for teaching them. Two listening tests have been standardized and are available for classroom use.³ There is still much to be done to spell out for teachers just what and how listening skills should be taught. A few school systems have attempted to do this, at least in part, in their language-arts guides. Denver has probably gone farther than any other school system in this regard. Denver school guides carefully outline listening skills to be taught and methods by which to teach them at each level, K–12.⁴

Although listening is by far the most extensively used of the four aspects of communication—reading, writing, listening, and speaking —research indicates that people listen at approximately a 25 per cent level of efficiency.⁵

Speaking. Two basic attitudes dominate the English area in regard to oral communication. The first maintains that speech should be left to the speech classes and is not an integral part of the English program. Reading and writing are so much more difficult and more vital than speaking for the educated person that instructional time and effort should be devoted to these skills. The other point of view maintains that speaking is so inextricably related to all forms of communication that it cannot be ignored in the study of language. Those who adhere to this view contend that speech has the power to sway men's minds, as dictators and demagogues demonstrate; that it also is the chief tool for the cooperative activity so necessary for reaching agreements and understanding among different national and international groups. Thus, because speech is so important to modern life, it should be included in all English programs. The latter point of view is the one taken by most leaders in English education and by the curriculum-makers.

Two kinds of speech activities are generally recommended and used: the formal speaker-audience situation, involving oral book reports, special reports, and oral compositions; and the informal give-and-take of conversation or discussion. The informal situation is emphasized because it is the more common mode of speech. Only on rather rare occasions do most people find themselves confronted

---

³ *Brown-Carlsen Listening Comprehension Test* (Tarrytown-on-Hudson, N.Y.: World Book Company, 1953).

Sequential Tests of Educational Progress: Listening Comprehension (Princeton, N.J.: Cooperative Test Division, Educational Testing Service, 1957).

⁴ *A Program in English* (Denver: The Department of Instruction, 1953).

⁵ Ralph G. Nichols and Leonard A. Stevens, *Are You Listening?* (New York: McGraw-Hill Book Company, Inc., 1957), p. ix.

with the task of making a formal presentation to an audience. Among the speech activities recommended by makers of English curriculum guides are discussing current topics, conducting meetings, reading aloud, making announcements, choral speaking, participating in panel discussions and symposiums, interviewing, and introducing speakers, to mention only a few. The topic of discussion is also important, for one of the chief responsibilities of the English teacher in relation to oral communication is to help young people realize the responsibility posed by the right of free speech. Unless the speaker displays basic integrity in his use of language, he prostitutes his freedom of speech. When this happens with any frequency, democracy itself is endangered. Thus both the "what" and the "how" of speech are of vital concern to any teacher who assumes the responsibility of developing communication skills in young people.

Grammar. Frequently *grammar* is used as a blanket term which includes such diversified skills as punctuation, usage, and even spelling. Grammarians, as well as those who are concerned with the teaching of language, define the term much more precisely. One textbook on the teaching of English defines it thus: "The systematic study of the relationship of words, clauses, and phrases within the English sentence."[6]

Nearly everyone agrees that some grammar should be taught in the secondary school. Beyond that there is wide diversity of thought on the "what," "why," and "how" of grammar. The traditionalists generally hold to the idea that English grammar should be based on Latin, taught by definition, and applied to unsnarling problems of written and spoken language.

The linguists or structuralists believe that the structure or patterning of every language is different, but contain some common elements. Thus, they see the structure or grammar of English as based not on Latin or German but, rather, on scientific analysis of the spoken language by linguistic scientists. These people contend that the structure of the English language should be taught inductively, starting with sentence patterns. The knowledge acquired is not to be used in the control of communication but as a basis for understanding the way our language operates.

Although the linguistic approach may never completely supplant

---

[6] Walter Loban, Margaret Ryan, and James R. Squire, *Teaching Language and Literature* (New York: Harcourt, Brace & World, Inc., 1961), p. 543.

the Latin-based grammar, the trend toward its use is growing stronger. Changes are being introduced in college English departments, by leaders in English education, by teachers who have glimpsed the possibilities in the newer approach, and by the linguistic scientists themselves. High school language texts are beginning to reflect this trend. Several series introduce the concept of sentence patterns and illustrate the basic patterns. Several also attempt the inductive approach, which is the principal method used by the linguists. Students build sentences; they seldom analyze a readymade sentence. One recognized linguist has written a detailed text for use in high schools which approaches the entire study of grammar from the point of view of linguistics.[7] What the future holds for the teaching of grammar is still uncertain, but that the teaching of grammar will change in many ways is abundantly clear.

Usage. To state that *it is me* is acceptable usage in the speech of educated people is no longer earth-shaking. Many English teachers accept the statement that there is no "right" or "wrong" language usage, but only usage that is appropriate or inappropriate in a given situation. Most language textbooks now explain usage in terms of levels. It is inappropriate for a student to use *ain't* in the classroom, but it may be quite appropriate on the playground or in his home. It is equally inappropriate when sincerely thanking one's hostess for a delicious dinner to speak of the *Epicurean repast of which I have partaken.* Flexibility of usage patterns and word choice is the key to language power. This is stressed in place of "right" or "wrong" standards.

On the other hand, although flexibility is the aim of usage study, a basic standard usage is important for every individual so that he can have some assurance that the way in which he expresses himself orally is acceptable to the educated ear. He must realize that there are individuals who will judge him by the way he speaks even before they hear what he has to say. This may be unfair, but it happens. The only way to avoid being misjudged because of inaccurate standard usage is to be so familiar with acceptable standard usage that it will come naturally when needed.

The acceptance of flexibility in language usage is not universal, of course. There are still many purists among teachers and other

---

[7] Paul Roberts, *English Sentences* (New York: Harcourt, Brace & World, Inc., 1962).

college graduates who believe that the English language is deteriorating and that the only way to keep it "pure" is to enforce rigorously the standards of correct English and to resist change in acceptable usage patterns. This group protested vigorously when *Webster's Third New International Dictionary of the English Language, Unabridged* was published because the editors had listed so many words, formerly considered slang, as colloquialisms and so many colloquialisms as standard, informal usage.

In spite of these people, change in a vital, growing language is inevitable. New words are added rapidly in this expanding culture as a result of the explosion of knowledge, and usage changes will continue to occur as long as we have a dynamic culture.

The trend in teaching usage, then, is toward more flexibility among levels with a sense of the appropriateness to a given situation plus an acceptance of informal standard usage as the language level suitable for the classroom.

Spelling. Spelling is a skill used in writing, and instruction in spelling should be closely related to all writing experiences. So much has been written and said about the lack of proficiency in spelling among high school graduates during the past forty years that literally hundreds of research projects have been devoted to studying aspects of spelling and relationships between spelling and other language skills. Some things have been learned from research, of course: for instance, there is wide variation in spelling proficiency among individuals; the most competent spellers are those who visualize readily; most people who have difficulty with spelling are kinesthetic spellers, those who learn to spell mainly through their muscles; 90 per cent of all spelling errors are found in 5000 basic words; unless the student wants to improve his spelling, no amount of drill will help him. But there are many research studies that appear to disagree as to whether regular spelling lessons or individualized spelling is more effective or whether the sound elements (phonics) of English are consistent enough to warrant concentrated work on them.

English teachers, by and large, teach spelling (in some form) throughout the junior high school years and some even in the senior high school. The poor showing made by students has not resulted from lack of attention to the problem but rather from the lack of consistency in putting teaching theory into practice. Sound psychological principles are too frequently ignored in relation to spelling.

There are some points on which authorities do agree; some of these points have come from research, others from careful observation of teaching-learning practices. For example, the poor speller often needs remedial attention: diagnosis of his difficulties and then prescribed work to overcome them. Anything less than this is usually useless. Some method of attacking the study of spelling should be thoroughly learned and used by the student. The individual must recognize that he has a responsibility to his readers to spell accurately. This is not an area for experimentation or invention, but for conformity. To be really effective, spelling grades should be given for everyday spelling in all kinds of writing situations—themes, essay tests, reports, answers to questions, and so forth—for the true test of spelling ability is in the writing the individual is called upon to do.

Vocabulary. Vocabulary is directly linked with experience. One is more likely to remember an experience if he has verbalized it. New experiences demand new vocabulary for comprehension and expression. Expanding vocabularies and expanding experiences go hand in hand; each is empty without the other.

The old method of assigning a given number of words to be looked up and then used in a sentence has no place in the modern psychology of learning. Words are learned best in context—the more dramatic the context, the more potent the meaning—not through memorizing definitions. Words chosen for special study should be introduced in a meaningful context. Most vocabulary development occurs subconsciously. One hears or sees an unfamiliar word in context and often is able to guess, with a high degree of accuracy, its meaning. Often one may be able to use words correctly in context and yet not be able to define them. This is the way connotations are developed—a necessary concept for language power.

Direct attack on vocabulary through use of the dictionary is useful, but it is only one method of obtaining information about a word. The dictionary is the last resort for most adults; they use it to verify or to unlock the meaning of a particularly difficult word. Teachers might take a clue from this behavior.

Some knowledge of prefix and suffix meanings can be helpful, but again this knowledge should be gained inductively so that the prefix *ex-*, for example, is associated with familiar words such as *exit, exterior,* or *exclude.* From examination of these known words and their meanings, the basic meaning of *ex-* as *out of* or *from* can be inferred, then tested against a new word such as *excommunicate.* Analysis and meaning must be linked with personal experience, either firsthand or vicarious, in order for power over words to be developed.

Spelling and vocabulary drills are frequently linked together. This often defeats the purpose of both. Only the already competent spellers benefit through vocabulary study, for the spelling of the words is no problem for them. The average or poor speller is frustrated on two counts: he neither understands nor uses the word; therefore he feels no need to learn to spell this particular word. Both skills need to be taught directly, but each needs its own special approach and setting.

Vocabulary-building is a skill that is difficult to teach because it is so infrequently understood. Yet it is basic to all language development—essential for expressing oneself adequately as well as for acquiring and expanding knowledge and information through reading and listening.

Proofreading. Many of the so-called composition errors are careless mistakes in punctuation and spelling which careful proofreading could eliminate. Much needless teaching of rules and unnecessary drill is found in classrooms where some practice in proofreading would have solved the problem more effectively. Children and young people (and sometimes adults, too) become so engrossed in putting down whatever they are trying to say that they neglect the niceties of punctuation or spelling. There is no harm in this, provided that—after the glow of creative inspiration has subsided—the writer goes back and rereads his manuscript, correcting it until it conforms with the expected standards. This is a procedure essential to accurate writing and one that can be taught in the classroom.

Mass media. During the past thirty years the mass media have become increasingly influential in the areas of usage and language patterns, cultural values, behavior patterns, and general information. Not all this influence on students is positive, when judged according to educational values. Teachers—English teachers especially—have become sufficiently concerned to incorporate studies of the various types of media into the curriculum. Units on "How to Read a Newspaper," "Evaluating Periodicals," or "The Benefits and Handicaps of Television" are frequently found in courses of study at the secondary level. The principal objective of these units is to help young people read and listen with more discrimination and to help them gain an appreciation for, and enjoyment from, worthwhile material.

Critical thinking can be and should be taught in relation to all the mass media. If a democratic society is to survive, it must educate its citizens to evaluate carefully what they see and hear—to accept nothing on face value until it has been carefully scrutinized. Without this kind of independent judgment on the part of individuals, it would be very easy for an individual or small group to gain control of the population through these media. It has happened elsewhere; it must not happen here. One way to produce critical thinkers is to deal directly with the products of the mass media in a constructive manner in the classroom.

Other Trends

There are several other trends apparent in the teaching and learning of English. These do not need elaboration here. In brief, they are:

1. An increased amount of fusion among the various aspects of the language arts; a closer working relationship among writing, mechanics, grammar, reading and literature, listening, speaking, and so forth;
2. A further striving to determine a scope and sequence for English based upon the developmental needs of young people, the demands of society for proficiency in language, and the nature of the language arts (this will not be accomplished easily nor quickly, but research is already being conducted to help give the program validity);
3. An increased emphasis on composition skills of all kinds and at every level;
4. More attention to wide reading as well as continued work on several carefully selected works read in common by the students;
5. An extensive use of thematic units, particularly in the junior high school.

These trends, as well as others, imply a needed strengthening of the teacher-education program for English teachers. More attention should be paid to the concepts of linguistic science and to the change which English has undergone and is undergoing. Greater emphasis on composition beyond the college freshman level is needed in the program for prospective English teachers, as well as attention to methods of teaching composition to secondary school students. It is difficult to teach composition if the teacher himself does not feel competent in this area. In addition, unless the teacher was a prolific reader himself between the ages of twelve and eighteen and has kept up with the dozens of new books for young people published every month since then, he needs special background in literature for the adolescent: what is available; how to motivate reading; how to teach taste and discrimination. The junior high school English teacher needs information on the needs and interests of adolescents and ways to make subject matter meaningful to them.

The teaching of English is a frightening as well as a challenging profession. All learning depends primarily on the ability of the individual to speak, to listen, to read, and to write. Without a competent mastery of his native tongue, the individual is forever handicapped. Thus, the English teacher is the person upon whom the success of the whole educational enterprise depends. This is a grave responsibility, yet one that cannot be shirked. To open the wide, wide world to young people, to help them understand themselves and others, to furnish them the tools for emotional release—these are the rewards as well as the responsibilities of the secondary school English teacher.

Bibliography

Association for Supervision and Curriculum Development, *Research Helps in Teaching the Language Arts.* Washington, D.C.: National Education Association, 1955.

Bruner, Jerome S., *The Process of Education.* Cambridge, Mass.: Harvard University Press, 1961.

Burton, Dwight L., *Literature Study in the High Schools,* rev. ed. New York: Holt, Rinehart & Winston, Inc., 1964.

Carlsen, G. Robert, "Conflicting Assumptions in the Teaching of English," *English Journal,* XLIX, 6 (September 1960), 377–86.

————, "Deep Down Where I Live," *English Journal,* XLIII, 5 (May 1954), 235–39.

————, "From High School into College," *English Journal,* XLV, 7 (October 1956), 400–405.

Commission on the English Curriculum, National Council of Teachers of English, *The English Language Arts.* New York: Appleton-Century-Crofts, Inc., 1952.

————, *The English Language Arts in the Secondary School.* New York: Appleton-Century-Crofts, Inc., 1956.

————, "Significance of the English Language Arts in the Secondary School: A Symposium," *English Journal,* XLVI, 5 (May 1957), 286–93.

Conant, James Bryant, *The American High School Today.* New York: McGraw-Hill Book Company, Inc., 1959.

————, *A Memorandum to School Boards: Recommendations for Education in the Junior High School Years.* Princeton, N.J.: Educational Testing Service, 1960.

Gray, William S., and Bernice Rogers, *Maturity in Reading: Its Nature and Appraisal.* Chicago: The University of Chicago Press, 1956.

Hanna, Geneva R., and Mariana K. McAllister, *Books, Young People, and Reading Guidance.* New York: Harper & Row, 1960.

Hook, J. N., *The Teaching of High School English,* 2nd ed. New York: The Ronald Press Company, 1959.

Jewett, Arno, *English Language Arts in American High Schools.* U.S. Office of Education Bulletin No. 13. Washington, D.C.: USGPO, 1958.

The Junior High School. State of Indiana Department of Public Instruction Bulletin No. 246. 1961. Pp. 22–26.

La Brant, Lou, "As of Now," *English Journal,* XLVIII, 6 (September 1959), 295–308.

————, *We Teach English.* New York: Harcourt, Brace & World, Inc., 1951.

Loban, Walter, Margaret Ryan, and James R. Squire, *Teaching Language and Literature.* New York: Harcourt, Brace & World, Inc., 1961.

McCullough, Constance, "What Does Research Reveal about Practices in Teaching Reading?" *English Journal,* XLVI, 8 (November 1957), 475–90.

Mearns, Hughes, *Creative Power: The Education of Youth in the Creative Arts,* 2nd rev. ed., New York: Dover Publications, Inc., 1958.

Norvell, George W., *The Reading Interests of Young People.* Boston: D. C. Heath & Company, 1950.

Pooley, Robert C. (ed.), *Perspectives on English.* New York: Appleton-Century-Crofts, Inc., 1960.

———, *Teaching English Grammar.* New York: Appleton-Century-Crofts, Inc., 1957.

———, *Teaching English Usage.* New York: Appleton-Century-Crofts, Inc., 1946.

Roberts, Paul, *English Sentences.* New York: Harcourt, Brace & World, Inc., 1962.

Rosenblatt, Louise, "Literature: The Reader's Role," *English Journal,* XLIX, 5 (May 1960), 15, 304–10.

Sauer, Edwin H., *English in the Secondary School.* New York: Holt, Rinehart & Winston, Inc., 1961.

Smith, Dora V., *Communication: The Miracle of Shared Living.* New York: The Macmillan Company, 1955.

Strom, Ingrid N., *The Implications of Research in Grammar for the Teaching of Writing.* Bulletin of the School of Education. Bloomington, Ind.: Indiana University, 1960.

Wilson, Margaret F., and J. Wesley Schneyer, *Developmental Reading in the Junior High School.* Philadelphia: University of Pennsylvania Educational Service Bureau, 1959.

Index

115